BALLERINA

BALLERINA

FASHION'S MODERN MUSE

PATRICIA MEARS

LAURA JACOBS

JANE PRITCHARD

ROSEMARY HARDEN

JOEL LOBENTHAL

VENDOME

NEW YORK · LONDON

CONTENTS

INTRODUCTION

PATRICIA MEARS

Back-stage, "Dancers of the American Ballet" with a visitor in a Saks Fifth Avenue corduroy suit. *Vogue*, September 1, 1937.

". . . the Russian Ballet, which, emerging in Paris in 1910, has had a profounder effect on the worlds of painting, music, fashion, and the decorative arts than any other single influence. . . . It has a glamour, a romantic pungency, unsurpassed by any other art form in that it excites the eye and the ear simultaneously and equally."[1]

This excerpt from an article that appeared in the November 1, 1933, issue of *Vogue* magazine encapsulates the extraordinary impact that the revolutionary Ballets Russes had on Western culture before and during the interwar years. Written by Lincoln Kirstein, the Harvard-educated aesthete who did as much as anyone to make New York City one of the premiere dance capitals of the twentieth century, the article was perhaps the first critical essay on classical ballet to appear in a leading American fashion magazine. Along with an eight-page photographic feature titled "The New Russian Ballet," published in *Vogue* the previous year, this article initiated regular coverage of the ballet in the popular fashion press for the next half century, particularly in the United States and Great Britain.

How and why did this centuries-old dance form and its most celebrated practitioners—ballerinas—begin to influence fashion in such profound and meaningful ways in the 1930s? And why did ballet culture soar in Great Britain and the United States, two Western countries with no previous ballet traditions? A primary objective of *Ballerina: Fashion's Modern Muse* is to provide answers to these compelling questions. Though the relationship between ballet and fashion is not a new topic, it has yet to be fully acknowledged and analyzed in depth.

Today, we take for granted that ballerinas have had a major impact on modern fashion. Even those who have never seen a ballet or have little knowledge of classical dance can readily recognize the key elements of the ballerina's professional raiment, whether for practice (knitted leotards and

legwarmers) or performance (fitted satin bodice and frothy tutu skirt, pink tights and satin pointe shoes). And most people are fully aware that a ballerina's costume encases a sleek, streamlined physique, from the top of her chignon-coiffed head to the tips of her articulated, pointed feet. Today, the ballerina is generally viewed as a respectable artist who dedicates her life to an endeavor that is as demanding as it is beautiful. This assessment, however, is a relatively recent phenomenon.

For most of ballet's long history, professional female dancers may have been lauded for their beauty and their skills but, with very few exceptions, were not viewed as proper ladies in society. In fact, many were culled from the lower classes and sexually exploited throughout their dancing careers. Ballerinas had little recourse to improve their lot, and most remained mute, like the art form itself (ballet dancers never speak, let alone sing, and rely entirely on physical movement and facial expression as their modes of communication). So it is not surprising that ballet's relationship with fashion has mostly been a one-sided affair. From its creation in the 1660s until the years prior to World War I, ballet

Edgar Degas, *The Rehearsal of the Ballet Onstage*, ca. 1874.

consistently reflected the latest fashion trends, but fashion rarely adapted elements from classical dance.

Although ballet was codified and professionalized in France in the mid-seventeenth century and was elevated to a supreme art form in Russia in the late nineteenth century, its popularization in the twentieth century owes much to the British and Americans. Both countries lacked the kind of governmental support and investment afforded dance companies and schools in countries like France, ballet's birthplace, Italy (mainly cities such as Naples and Milan), Denmark, and, of course, Russia. The absence of state-sponsored companies in Great Britain and the United States meant that until the 1930s, ballet was frequently viewed as a form of entertainment for the masses. Then, quite suddenly, Britain and America embraced ballet. The intelligentsia, socialites, artists, writers, and the lower classes alike began flocking to performances, and before long, favorite ballerinas became revered figures in a newly respected art form.

It is somewhat ironic that two of the most important nations in ballet's history, France and Russia, played a lesser role in the glorification of modern ballet. By the interwar years of the twentieth century, France's influence had diminished significantly. The heyday of the Romantic-era ballerina, born on Parisian stages, began to fade as early as the mid-nineteenth century. Even before the 1870s, when ballet dancers' meager lives were immortalized in the works of French Impressionist painter Edgar Degas, they were thought to be little more than artistically trained prostitutes, readily available to the wealthy, domineering patrons (called *abonnés* of the Jockey Club) of the opera and ballet. So powerful were the *abonnés* that they required all operas performed at the Paris Opéra to include a ballet so the male attendees could ogle the young female dancers. Perhaps it is not surprising that the ballerina's calf-length costume, a decided departure from anything worn in society, high or low, symbolized not only femininity and dynamic artistry but also sexual availability. Called the *tutu*, the name was a corruption of the crude French street expression *cucu*, or *petit cul* (the behind). Some members of the ballet audience—those in the cheaper seats located in the lower part of the theater, rather than the more

elite patrons who occupied the elevated boxes ringing the auditorium—had a particularly revealing view of the dancers. From the "pit," one could catch occasional glimpses up the ballerinas' skirts. Thus, *cucu* eventually transformed into "tutu."

The decline of ballet in France was counterbalanced by its majestic rise in Imperial Russia. From the 1880s to the onset of the Russian Revolution in 1917, many of the most famous and celebrated ballets in history were created, and the style of Russian ballet was exquisitely honed. After the revolution, a steady stream of that nation's greatest artists migrated to the West. Their talent, technical training, and knowledge of the great Russian ballets became the foundation upon which Great Britain and the United States built their temples of dance. Émigrés such as Sergei Diaghilev (1872–1929), the legendary impresario who brought the Ballets Russes to the West in 1909 and led the company until his death, and Anna Pavlova (1881–1931), the most famous ballerina of her age, insured that Imperial Russian classical ballet would not only survive but would also evolve into the most popular performing art in Great Britain in the 1930s and 1940s, and later in the United States.

In Soviet Russia, ballet remained a politically important art form throughout the twentieth century. Its modernization, however, was evident more in the impeccable training of its dancers than in choreographic advancement or experimentation. Despite disparities in innovation, several key aspects of Russian and Western ballet developed in a more or less parallel manner. Among them was the ballerina's physique. Like high-fashion models, ballerinas on both sides of the Iron Curtain became increasingly slender. Soviet dancers may have had little access to the latest modes or fashion images, but their striving for technical virtuosity—to jump higher and spin faster—required leaner, more articulated bodies. During the Cold War, cultural exchanges brought Soviet ballet companies to the West. Their ballerinas had a tremendous influence on Western dance, but on little else.

In contrast, when British and American classical ballet took its place in the pantheon of modern high culture in the West, it asserted a profound influence on other fields of creativity, fashion chief among them. Home-grown ballerinas

blossomed into revered and aspirational figures of beauty and glamour, and their signature costume—the corseted tutu—inspired many of fashion's leading designers. From the interwar years through the mid-century, haute couture turned to classical ballets such as *Giselle*, *Swan Lake*, and *The Sleeping Beauty* for stylistic and aesthetic inspiration.

Numerous books and articles have documented how works by the Ballets Russes inspired Parisian couture after the company's breathtaking debut in 1909. For example, "exotic" productions such as *Scheherazade* are credited with igniting the craze for Orientalist-style turbans, harem pants,

and tunics made with vibrantly colored fabrics just before the onset of World War I. Only the faintest trace of the tutu, however, could be detected in the fashions of the era.

By the 1930s, the craze for ballet, or "balletomania," as it was called by some, was both widespread and profound. Fashion high and low mirrored the rise of classical ballet in the West, and the two were often intertwined, as the resurgence of Romantic and Victorian modes echoed stagings of full-length, classical Russian ballets, as well as voluptuous new productions. Fashion magazines also presented whimsical and unique ballet features that actively engaged their

ABOVE: "Do You Know Your Ballets?" British *Vogue*, September 1, 1937. Silhouettes of *Boutique Fantasque*, *Scheherazade*, *Les Cents Baisers*, *Petroushka*, and *Tricorne* by Lotte Reiniger. OPPOSITE: Ballet-inspired holiday cover, *Vogue*, December 1, 1920.

The Vogue Company
CONDÉ NAST, Publisher

readers. For example, the September 1, 1937, issue of British *Vogue* included a two-page editorial spread entitled "Do You Know Your Ballets?" It was a quiz consisting of ten groupings of costumed dancers charmingly rendered in silhouette, a technique popular during the Romantic era, by Lotte Reiniger, with a key identifying the ballets printed in the back of the issue. The text that accompanied the silhouettes summarized the impact of that season's ballet performances:

> Balletomaniacs flit once more through the foyer at Covent Garden, tense with culture, shrill with opinion. No pastime this; it becomes almost as serious as sport. The gallery fans are pressed together like caviare [*sic*]: as the curtain falls they yowl their plaudits and clatter out to surge round the stage door, awaiting their disen-tu-tu'ed divinities. And you, dear reader, will you be among them?... Or will you join that eclectic band of influential personages who nightly trail their grandeur through the pass-door, on to the dusty, deserted stage, tracking the Tartar to its lair, peeping behind the scenes, sniffing the grease paint like old war horses... loud with recollection of a Diaghilevian hey-dey.[2]

About 1932, articles on classical ballet began to appear regularly in leading fashion magazines such as *Vogue* and *Harper's Bazaar*. By the late 1930s and throughout World War II, ballerinas were regularly featured models in fashion editorials. In the same issues, dance coverage abounded, a phenomenon that continued for the next several decades. Goods from stockings to nightgowns were advertised using ballerinas or packaged with balletic elements, clearly drawing a connection between these products and the elegant qualities of classical dance. Meanwhile, fashion designers in Paris, London, and New York freely adapted elements of the ballet costume into their work, and some even designed dance costumes and sets; all of it was widely covered in fashion publications.

This interrelationship between ballet and fashion reached its peak from the late 1940s through the 1950s. Couturiers such as Pierre Balmain, Christian Dior (who dressed ballerinas Margot Fonteyn, Maria Tallchief, and Ruth Page), and

Charles James simultaneously created ballet-inspired gowns featuring boned bodices and voluminous tulle skirts and ballet costumes for the stage. At the same time, American ready-to-wear designers made knitted separates and wrap dresses that were reminiscent of leotards and other ballet practice clothing worn by dancers in class or in rehearsal. Claire McCardell, one of the greatest fashion designers in American history, is credited with being the first to pair actual ballet slippers with her innovative garments.

Ballet's sway on fashion slowly began to diminish in the 1960s. Its great mid-century influence waned with the rise of youth culture and the simultaneous decline of high fashion. Like haute couture, ballet's glamour and creativity, so vital during the hardships of the Depression, World War II, and the Cold War, eroded as the tumultuous counterculture swelled. The increasingly relaxed and eclectic dress code was a rejection of aspirational formality. The fashion world's interest in ballet has been revived since the advent of the new millennium, but this period will not be covered in depth in this book.

Rather, this book focuses on the golden age of ballet's influence on fashion—from the early 1930s through the late 1970s—when ballet fever was at its apogee in Great Britain and the United States. To understand how a few star ballerinas created the template for modern performers to influence and use fashion to their advantage, two of the essays look back at the transformation of ballet from a male- to a female-dominated art form during the nineteenth century.

Most of the book documents three primary ways ballet and select ballerinas impacted modern fashion. One was the creation of fashionable clothing, from haute couture to ready-to-wear, that echoed the look of the ballerina, especially her tutu, but also her jewelry, satin pointe shoes and slippers, and leotards. The second was the consistent and wide-ranging visual exposure of the ballerina in popular-culture arenas, such as fashion magazines, films, and theater. And the third was the offstage aura of ballerinas as women of style. Most dancers did not have the wherewithal to wear high fashion. But many had the motivation to dress stylishly, and a lucky few took advantage of their fortuitous wealth to acquire notable couture garments. Together, these dancers burnished the

Ballet Russe de Monte Carlo dancers Irina Baronova and Nini Theilade in dresses by B. Altman. *Harper's Bazaar*, May 1940.

notion of the ballerina as an aspirational figure to be emulated by all classes of women.

Although the primary focus of this book is narrow in scope and time, the subject is interconnected with many other disciplines. Therefore, though it follows a more or less chronological trajectory, many of the same themes—fashion's adaptation of the ballerina's habiliment and the ballerina as model and woman of style—weave fluidly from chapter to chapter and across time and geography. It is worth noting that this is not an in-depth study of classical ballet. While the two fashion curators include a great deal of information about ballet in their essays, it is the three dance specialists whose contributions provide the necessary scholarship.

In the lead essay, the critic Laura Jacobs analyzes the unique position of the ballerina within a culture and a country, exploring what it means when we bestow the title of ballerina upon a classical dancer. What is expected of this woman physically, theatrically, and poetically, and has the definition changed over time? Jacobs, who has written extensively about dance, theater, and fashion, is uniquely qualified to tackle this subject.

Next is a compelling essay documenting the development of the ballet costume in Western Europe throughout the nineteenth century. Written by Jane Pritchard, one of the world's leading dance curators, it traces the stylistic evolution of ballerinas' stage bodices, skirts, and hairstyles, all of which mirrored fashionable dress, particularly evening wear. Pritchard also focuses on the rise of costumiers, who, like their fashion counterparts, grew steadily in number and influence as urban development exploded and theaters proliferated.

My first essay documents the rise of the fashionable ballerina. After a glimpse at the earliest female stars of the Baroque and Rococo periods, it focuses on the impact of the greatest Romantic-era ballerina, Marie Taglioni. Her career and public persona became the template for subsequent generations of female dancers and is therefore crucial to understanding how audiences, particularly women, came to revere ballerinas. Taglioni's heir was Anna Pavlova, *the* modern ballerina, who had a profound influence on the aesthetics of dance and fashion. She traveled more than 300,000 miles,

dancing around the world on any stage available to her, thus becoming the most widely recognizable dancer of her age, if not in history. Her dark, soulful features and lithesome physique may have been antithetical to the prevailing aesthetics when she began her dance training, but thousands of carefully crafted photographs of her in costumes and couture were globally distributed, thus imprinting the image of the ballerina on generations of dance fans and casual viewers alike.

My second essay explores the period when fashion clearly and irrevocably took its inspiration from classical ballet. This golden age began with the rise of ballet culture in Great Britain during the 1920s, its interrelationship with Russian émigrés based in England and France, and the interplay between haute couture and ballet costume design, which paralleled the burgeoning neo-romantic style. A few random examples of delicately embroidered tulle and panniered gowns were created in the 1920s, a look that became a fashion mainstay during the 1930s and continued for the next two decades. The text details Parisian couture's consistent reliance on ballet as the art form expanded around the world, with fashion publications and ballet-inspired films serving as catalysts to promote and encourage the interaction between the two disciplines.

The next two essays focus on mid-century ballerinas: one is about Margot Fonteyn of England's Royal Ballet; the other details the first generation of New York City Ballet dancers, especially Tanaquil Le Clercq. They became stars of the stage as well as the physical embodiments of what many believed a ballerina should look like. Fashion curator Rosemary Harden's essay illuminates how the regally cool Fonteyn amassed her enviable haute couture wardrobe while performing around the world. The collection Harden oversees, housed in the Fashion Museum in Bath, England, is home to many of Fonteyn's couture treasures, which were designed primarily by Christian Dior and Yves Saint Laurent.

On the other side of the Atlantic, the leggy and glamorous Tanaquil Le Clercq was the ideal American beauty. She and such colleagues as Maria Tallchief and Melissa Hayden lit up the stage in works by George Balanchine, while fashionable images of Le Clercq graced the pages of fashion magazines.

New York City Ballet (NYCB) ballerina Lauren Lovette in Maggie Norris's "Angelique" gold-embroidered corset and tulle skirt, 2012.

Joel Lobenthal, a noted dance and fashion writer, critic, and historian, describes these "dryads" and their relationship to, and impact on, fashion and style, both on and off the stage.

The final chapters of the book focus on the interplay between modern ballet and fashion in America from the 1940s through the 1970s. After immigrating to the United States, Russian-born Balanchine developed a new style of choreography—sleek, fast, musical, and often plotless—with the streamlined dancer in mind. Many of his ballerinas looked like the emerging generation of American models, who were becoming taller and thinner. And stage costumes became more and more pared down. Indeed, a number of Balanchine's most celebrated masterpieces were performed in knitted leotards and tights. These "black-and-white ballets," as they were called, reflected and perhaps influenced the clothing that American designers excelled at, mainly sportswear and functional separates. Many of the best creators were women who made garments that had more in common with ballet practice and rehearsal clothing than with tutus. Included is an analysis of two leading New York City Ballet dancers, Allegra Kent and Mimi Paul, the most frequently featured ballerina models in *Harper's Bazaar* and *Vogue* in the 1960s.

It is perhaps ironic that fashion took so long to adapt elements of ballet attire, as both art forms rely on the human physique as a point of departure for their creative expression. Ballerinas, who had been looked down upon and exploited for so long, benefited from shifting cultural winds that elevated their art and their position in society. So powerful was ballet's modern incarnation that the historical disrepute of ballerinas was banished during the interwar years of the twentieth century. Revering ballerinas, fashion's modern muses, continues to this day.

NYCB ballerina Lauren Lovette in Victor de Souza's white satin and black tulle corset and bolero, 2016.

CROWN JEWELS

LAURA JACOBS

'Tis little I — could care for Pearls —
Who own the ample sea —
Or Brooches — when the Emperor —
With Rubies — pelteth me —

Or Gold — who am the Prince of Mines —
Or Diamonds — when have I
A Diadem to fit a Dome —
Continual upon me —

Emily Dickinson, No. 466

In the poem "'Tis little I—could care for Pearls," written in 1862, Emily Dickinson positions the artist as the richest of royals. Earthly treasures, those brooches and baubles bought at Cartier and Fabergé, are nothing compared to the imagination's vast seas and deep mines, a kingdom of boundless wealth. Queens and their daughters may regularly wear diadems, but they measure only the circumference of their heads and the size of their country. Dickinson's diadem fits a "Dome"—the celestial sphere above and around us—and its diamonds are the stars in the sky. Indeed, Dickinson could easily be describing that artist we call a ballerina, whose body is trained on circlets, halos, and hemispheres, and whose serene power feels supreme. Though it isn't quite possible to pinpoint the moment that the ballerina's reign began, three or so centuries ago, it has ever since been continual.

Cloistered in Amherst, Massachusetts, fiercely interior, Dickinson never attended the ballet. But she did read the illustrated papers, which contained reviews of theater, opera, and, yes, classical dance. Another of her poems of 1862, "I cannot dance upon my Toes," is intriguingly conversant with ballet and its vocabulary. Dickinson uses the terms *pirouette* and *prima*. She cites the ballerina's "Gown of Gauze" and "Ringlet" headpiece. And in comparing dancers to "Birds, / One Claw upon the Air," she describes the position we know as arabesque. More fascinating still, "I cannot dance upon my Toes" was Dickinson's written answer—or rather, roguish rebuke—to her literary mentor, Thomas Wentworth Higginson, who had suggested that she should construct her poetry more conventionally, with less rupture—and rapture!—between

words and phrases. "No Man instructed me," the poem states, Dickinson's way of saying that she hasn't been academically trained and will not toe the traditional line. And yet, by the end of this mischievous poem, no doubt written at the poet's small square desk, her hair parted down the middle, each side curving low over her ears in the style of nineteenth-century Romanticism, Dickinson herself is the ballerina.

So the term *ballerina* has two levels of meaning—prosaic and poetic. The prosaic assumes a daily classical training of many years and a mastery of pointe work, i.e., dancing upon the toes. Merriam-Webster states that a ballerina is "a woman who is a ballet dancer," a vague definition that includes just about any female in pointe shoes, from advanced student to corps member to soloist to star. This is a very broad brush. Experienced fans of the art form use the term with much more discernment.

The nineteenth-century artist Edgar Degas, for instance, in over one thousand renderings of life backstage, onstage, and in the studios of the Paris Opera Ballet, did not refer to his subjects as ballerinas. He called them "dancers." Despite the alchemizing heat of the footlights, which gave a blissful glow to their faces and made gossamer their costumes of tulle, he saw these young women as human form, concentrated endeavor, and prey, the potential conquests of deep-pocketed men in white tie, the Jockey Club gents. Like Marie Geneviève van Goethem, the model for Degas's famous sculpture—*Little Dancer of Fourteen Years*—these hungry, hardworking ballet girls, the youngest of them referred to as *les petits rats*, often disappeared into the Parisian demimonde. Or into poverty.

Then again, Degas's subject usually wasn't the top of the roster; it was more often the corps de ballet—the rank-and-file females who comprise the body and breath of a ballet company, few of whom climb higher. The rigor and anonymity of the corps absorbed Degas. He captured flares of elation in pastel plumes of light, and with brackish shadows he suggested the uncertain fate of girls faceless in the wings. As a dancer moved up from the corps de ballet to soloist status, or higher still to what the French continue to call *étoile*, or "star," she became less vulnerable, more autonomous and singular. It is the women at the top of the roster who are the ballerinas. Put

PRECEDING PAGES: NYCB ballerina Suzanne Farrell costumed for "Diamonds," the third act of George Balanchine's *Jewels*, 1967.

another way, as Mary Clarke and Clement Crisp have written, "The ballerina is the figure who is traditionally the pinnacle of the ballet—that is, dance in its most refined and elitist form."[1]

Even here, further distinction was once made. Back in the nineteenth century and into the twentieth, two honorifics set a handful of ballerinas apart from their sisters—titles that even Emily Dickinson knew about. When she drops the word *Prima* into her ballet poem of 1862, she is referring to a "prima ballerina," one whose artistry and authority place her "first" among her peers. Even higher than the prima was the "prima ballerina assoluta." *Assoluta* means "absolute, unquestionable." This title, rarely given, acknowledged a prima ballerina later in life, after a long career of international renown.

How did these honorifics come to a dancer? The process was inconsistent and unclear. The company, the government,

a monarch could dub thee prima ballerina or prima ballerina assoluta—sometimes stepping on toes. When the Mariinsky Theater ballerina Matihlde Kschessinska received the title of prima, in 1896, it came to her not through Marius Petipa, the august Mariinsky director, but through the Imperial Russian court, with which she was intimately connected (she'd been the mistress of Tsarevich Nikolai, son of Alexander III, emperor of Russia, and had a child with one of Nikolai's cousins).[2] Kschessinska *was* a gifted ballerina, but Petipa disapproved of her political path to prima. Today, these two honorifics are outmoded.

In our non-hierarchical times, the top-tier women and men in a ballet company are called principal dancers. This doesn't mean that the ballerina isn't alive and well. It means that it is up to us, each of us for ourselves, to decide which principal women are true ballerinas. Who pulls a stole of

Edgar Degas, *Ballet Scene (Scène de ballet)*, pastel over monotype on paper, ca. 1879.

atmosphere, her own imaginative realm, about her shoulders? Who transfixes us with her wanderings inside the music, taking us places no one has before? Who makes us sit up straight, teasing us with her inflections, making law of her whims? Who throws thunderbolts from Mount Olympus or flies straight into the sun on wings that do not melt? And who surprises us always, with her tenderness or delicacy or bravery or wit? All principal dancers are expected to fulfill the requirements of a role with accomplished technique and theatrical know-how. But the ballerina takes poetic possession of a role. She is responsible for the ballet—a domain she carries, or rules, effortlessly. There may not be a fixed, officially designated number of ballerinas, but all who follow classical dance will have a personal list, one that may even include a soloist or two, as well as a ballerina-to-be levitating in the corps.

In 1939 Lincoln Kirstein, the brilliant arts impresario who partnered with choreographer George Balanchine to co-found the New York City Ballet, published a little ballet dictionary called *Ballet Alphabet.* His definition of ballerina was workaday, except for its sweeping final phrase. It reads: "Originally an Italian word meaning girl-dancer. It has come to signify in every western tongue an outstanding female soloist in a traveling company, a ranking principal in an opera-house, as well as a symbol for the whole of classical dancing."[5]

A symbol, then. And as we read earlier, a pinnacle.

Think of the tiny ballerina that is poised—two inches tall and wearing a tutu—inside a child's pink jewelry box. When the lid is opened, the ballerina spins, usually to music by Tchaikovsky, her pirouette reflected in a small mirror. How many of the countless young recipients of these charming boxes, one wonders, has actually seen a ballet? And does it matter? It is instinctively understood that this figure, statuesque and solitary in a cozy theater of melody and velvet, exists outside everyday norms and simultaneously inside the imagination—the box! Just as nestlings are born knowing the meaning of certain silhouettes overhead, so this silhouette is accepted as one that quite naturally presides over a realm of riches, because she herself is a kind of jewel—a multifaceted sum of movement, music, sculpture, theater, poetry, and Apollonian

energy gathered in one artist. Crystalizing her culture, she is pure expression—minus speech—and this makes her symbolic.

Consider one of the greatest artists of the twentieth century, a man who was obsessed not with dancers, but with ballerinas—the pinnacle! His name was Joseph Cornell, and in the mid-twentieth century he constructed hundreds of boxes that were makeshift theaters of the mind and soul. Like Emily Dickinson, he was solitary and increasingly reclusive. But he had epiphanies and passions, which he pursued in his boxes, and one of these was ballerinas. Three times Cornell saw the incomparable Anna Pavlova dance during her farewell tour of 1924–25. In 1940 he met Tamara Toumanova—the "Black Pearl of the Russian Ballet"—a raven-haired beauty who'd been one of the three famous "baby ballerinas," a trio of precocious teens that intrigued audiences of the early 1930s. A bit later Cornell saw and met the effervescent French ballerina Renée "Zizi" Jeanmaire, a bubble of Veuve Clicquot. In the 1960s he found friendly affinity with the fey and wayward spirit Allegra Kent, Balanchine's most unpossessible muse at the New York City Ballet.

Cornell was a studious fan. He went to the ballet, wrote about it, kept up with its costume and set design, and delved into its history. Because of this delving, which he called "exploring," he was as obsessed with ballerinas of the past as he was with those of the present, perhaps more so. The Romantic ballerinas Marie Taglioni, Lucile Grahn, Fanny Elssler, Carlotta Grisi, and Fanny Cerrito—heroines in an era that saw the male dancer's bravado rendered ridiculous when compared to the ballerina's weightless virtuosity, her new reach into netherworlds of existential complexity—all were subjects of Cornell boxes. Cerrito, in her role as Ondine in 1843—the water sprite envisioned by Friedrich, Baron de la Motte Fouqué in his short novel of 1811, *Undine*—most of all.

Women of the water have long been symbols of the subconscious, hybrids swimming between states of being—reality and dream, matter and myth, consciousness and the unconscious. Ondine, the water sprite with a human form, longs for a soul, yet her kiss can kill. In *The Little Mermaid*, Hans Christian Andersen's story of 1836, the mermaid longs for both body and soul so that she may marry the human she

Joseph Cornell, *Untitled [Tamara Toumanova]*, collage with tempera on paperboard, ca. 1940.

ABOVE: Joseph Cornell, *Untitled [Zizi Jeanmaire Lobster Ballet]*, box construction, ca. 1949.
OPPOSITE: A. E. Chalon, *Pas de Quatre*, lithograph, ca. 1845. Left to right: Carlotta Grisi, Marie Taglioni, Lucile Grahn, and Fanny Cerrito.

loves. Asking the Sea Witch to transform her fishtail into legs and feet, she is told she must give up her voice in exchange. This paradigm speaks eloquently to the dancer. The word-lessness of the ballerina is part of her physical containment and grace. It has certainly kept her mystery intact in a world that grows ever more verbally cacophonous. Mid-century peers Margot Fonteyn and Zizi Jeanmaire, respectively and memorably, danced Ondine and the Little Mermaid. The ballet "Emeralds," the first act of Balanchine's full-length triptych *Jewels*, leads us into a floating medieval dream world as if through blue-green waters. And back in 1841, the Wilis of *Giselle* were drawn from Heinrich Heine's description of "elves in white dresses, whose hems are always damp."

But what did the ballerina embody for Cornell? Lyricism that finds expression not in sound but in limbs arranged spatially. Meaning that swims to the surface and then disappears, sometimes forever. A fluid physicality that is creaturely and yet human. "She's like a whale in her own ocean," Balanchine was heard to say while watching his last muse, the ballerina Suzanne Farrell, dancing the magisterial white-tutu role of "Diamonds," the third act of *Jewels* ("Rubies" is in the middle).[4]

Taking note of the other explorations that Cornell pursued in his boxes allows us to place the ballerina in a shared habitat. Cornell loved birds, from bright warblers to exotic parrots to nocturnal owls niched in shadow. He was compelled by Medici princes and princesses, by hotels and celestial maps, by rough-hewn dovecotes and handsome palaces. All of these themes, in one way or another, express migration and dislocation, nobility and eternity, transience and transport. Cornell understood that the ballerina was less a person than a meta-physical entity—or deity—her dimensions deepening and enlarging with every role she danced. The rarified air in his magical, glass-fronted spaces—this is the air she breathes.

Air, of course, is the ballerina's primary element. From ballet's beginning, which technically dates to 1661, when King Louis XIV oversaw the founding of France's Royal Academy of Dance, lift was built quite consciously into the classical technique.[5] The dancer strove for placement that was light yet plumb. Weight was balanced in the ball of the foot, never

settling in the heel; the derriere was pulled in; the breastbone and head were in regal league with the sun above. Upward momentum, vertical mobility—the art's lexicon of steps, jumps, and leaps aimed ever higher. In 1832, when the ballerina Marie Taglioni rose to pointe in the ballet *La Sylphide*, it was neuromuscular logic and aesthetic fulfillment at once. Suddenly the ballerina existed in a higher sphere, her connection to the earth seemingly one of choice rather than necessity. Pointe opened up a whole new dimension—a metaphorical plane—that offered entry into myriad states of being. It took the female, and the art form, to a place the male dancer could not follow.

La Sylphide was custom made for Marie by her father, the choreographer Filippo Taglioni. A sylphide (or sylph) is a sort of wood nymph, winged and capricious, her energy benevolent yet wayward. Filippo Taglioni used this role to frame his daughter's unique gifts of featherweight lightness and soaring ballon, the attenuated line of her low shoulders and long arms, and her ability to take a breath, a momentary pause, on the tips of her very strong toes. The theatrical charge of this ethereal being captivated audiences everywhere.

Furthermore, as the British historian Cyril Beaumont writes, "*La Sylphide* also marks a revolution in stage costume." Sylphs had been depicted onstage before 1832, but in high-waisted Regency costume, tunics that followed the figure. "The new dress of the new Sylphide," Beaumont explains, "created by Eugène Lami alone or in collaboration with Taglioni herself, was designed not to *display* the lines of the body, but to *conceal* them by means of a milky haze." Here was the classic Romantic tutu: a tight-fitting bodice, a bell-shaped skirt. "It is said," Beaumont continues, "that the actual color of the dress was not white, but a faintly bluish tint to suggest the clouds which were the Sylphide's domain. It may be, but in the gaslight of the stage the costume appeared white."[6]

The influence of Taglioni's sylph—her heightened sighs on pointe, her skirt of vapor—was enormous. Composers, virtuosos, and playwrights paid homage to her. She "inspired the dreams of poets," the Russian critic André Levinson writes in his book *Marie Taglioni*.[7] A taste for the luminous *ballet blanc* (white ballet), once created, demanded to be fed. "After

British ballerina Margot Fonteyn as the water sprite in Frederick Ashton's *Ondine*, a three-act ballet that premiered in 1958.

hummingbird's blur. Paired with bodices of satin or damask—fabrics as iridescent as a beetle's shell casings, or glittering as with dewdrops, diamonds—there is always something of Cinderella's metamorphosis about the ballerina's tutu. It is both mist and crinoline, cloud and gown, not one or the other but something in between. In *Giselle*, the ghostly glamour of the act two Wilis in their white tulle has the property of ectoplasm—a substance or spiritual energy.

Gelsey Kirkland, a purist preparing for her New York debut in *Giselle* in 1975, was entranced by the moth-like tutu that the Italian ballerina Carla Fracci wore in act two, when Giselle emerges as a newborn Wili. "The material flowed," Kirkland writes in her memoir, *Dancing on My Grave*, "the hem was frayed, radiating behind her body like a soft flame." Kirkland asked Fracci where she might get a tutu just like it, and Fracci demurred. "I buy from a little old man," she said. "But he stop making." It was ever thus; ballerinas are like goddesses on Mount Olympus, competitive even on a good day. But Kirkland was not to be put off. She stole into Fracci's dressing room and snipped a small sample, the size of a quarter, from the costume's inner layer. Its secret? The tutu was made of 100 percent silk tulle, far more extravagant and expensive than tulle of nylon, polyester, or rayon—and far more alive. With no regrets, Kirkland spent a thousand dollars on her own silk tutu.[9] In a short film clip of her first solo in act two, that tutu wreathes around her like a whirlwind of frost.

Tulle is volatile matter. In the nineteenth century, lofting too close to gas jets, too many tutus burst into flame. Most famous was the loss of Emma Livry, a protégé of Marie Taglioni who shared Taglioni's gift of ineffable ballon. In 1860 Taglioni created a signature ballet, *Le Papillon*, for Livry, who danced the role of Farfalla, a young woman magically turned into a butterfly. Near the ballet's end, when Farfalla singes her wings in the glow of a torch, the spell loosens and she regains her human form. This happy ending contained a terrible clairvoyance, for in 1862 Livry did more than singe her wings. Backstage, preparing for her entrance in *La Muette de Portici*, she fluffed her skirts near a low-hanging gaslight and they instantly ignited. The gentle Livry died of her burns eight months later. Fire is not the

La Sylphide," the French critic Théophile Gautier famously wrote, in 1844, "the scene-painters received orders only for romantic forests, valleys illuminated by the pretty German moonlight reminiscent of Heinrich Heine's ballads. . . . The new style led to a great abuse of white gauze, tulle, and tarlatan; the shades dissolved into mist by means of transparent dresses. White was the only color used."[8]

Tulle, which is thought to have originated in the city of Tulle in central France, became the ballerina's raiment, a netting in which warp and weft are twisted to form a state of tension—a weave of tiny hexagons. Tulle is a honeycomb of air, and it allies ballet dancers with those winged sisterhoods of eternal purpose. Is not the queen bee the ballerina of the hive? Tulle floats and rests like a butterfly's wings, a

Italian ballerina Carla Fracci in *Giselle*, costumed as a Wili, ca. 1969.

ballerina's element, though she may dance with heat or temper. Classical dance is water and air.[10]

I have used the phrase "states of being" twice in this essay, and the ballerina is indeed, ballet to ballet, a form of energy that moves from one state or shape to another. Entomology, ornithology, and folklore, species both natural and supernatural—swans, horses, fairies, furies, sylphs, Wilis, undines, unicorns—the ballerina endows these many morphologies with a soul.

At the same time, however, she is a silent ambassador of the state—the country that nurtured her to ballerinadom and of which she is the most cultivated of its treasures. For above all the ballerina represents her native soil. Her national identity begins in ballet class with first position, because each country brings its own aesthetic values, historical muscle memory, and distinct musicality to its classical training and dancing. Many would argue, as has August Bournonville, the great Danish choreographer and ballet master, that there is a moral dimension to these values, memories, and musical responses. He believed classical dancing was "an important factor in the spiritual development of the nation."[11] It is the ballerina who embodies a country's unwritten ideal of grace in all its meanings.

The girlishly sacrificial grandeur of the Soviet Union's Galina Ulanova. The golden mean of Margot Fonteyn, emblematic of England's sense of correctness and proportion. Maria Tallchief—half Irish, half Osage Indian—America's first approximation of a "prima ballerina," her crowning glory a cantilena line that seemed to listen to the land. These three mid-century ballerinas are go-to examples of dancing definitive of birthplace. Others leap to mind . . . The sfumato softness and line of Italy's Carla Fracci, a quattrocento principessa. The impish delight of Lis Jeppesen, a delicate Thumbelina from the storied Danes. The elegantly enunciated classicism of Élisabeth Platel, a French lesson in purity of presentation. Suzanne Farrell's extreme transparency, an American classicism porous and powerful. Veronika Part's sensual St. Petersburg perfection—part Snow Maiden, part Anna Karenina. The list goes on and on.

And so does the ballerina's hold on us.

American ballerina Gelsey Kirkland in *Giselle*, costumed as a Wili, with Mikhail Baryshnikov, 1975.

Why did George Balanchine call his plotless masterpiece of 1967 *Jewels*? Well, there's the Cluny unicorn tapestry, the sixth—titled *À Mon Seul Désir*—from which Balanchine took inspiration: it shows a women holding a necklace over a jewel box.[12] The ballet is fixed in an era of chivalry, a time that saw noblewomen adorned with gems. And watching the ballet, one feels that Balanchine is leading us through the faceted echo chamber of each cut stone—an emerald, a ruby, a diamond. Yes, Barbara Karinska's spectacular green, red, and white tutus glitter with paste embellishment, but more than that, each act brims with allusions to Arthurian ardor and enchanted creatures, while refracting aspects of the great nineteenth-century ballets. This work of Symbolist imagery communicates on many levels at once, keeps beguiling secrets, and holds shimmering emotional depths. Only one thing is absolutely clear. The ballerinas are the jewels.

ABOVE: *À Mon Seul Désir*, the sixth tapestry in *The Lady with the Unicorn* series, ca. 1480–90, Musée de Cluny, Paris. OPPOSITE: George Balanchine and the gems in *Jewels*, choreography by George Balanchine (New York), 1967. Clockwise from left: Mimi Paul, Violette Verdy, Patricia McBride, and Suzanne Farrell.

FASHION AND DANCE COSTUME IN THE NINETEENTH CENTURY

JANE PRITCHARD

"First draw me the form of a woman as it is in Nature. And now draw me the form of a woman in a modern corset and the satin slippers used by our modern dancers. Now do you not see that the movement that would conform to one figure would be perfectly impossible for the other?" Isadora Duncan's words at the turn of the nineteenth into the twentieth century serve as a useful reminder of the restrictive nature of the costumes worn by female ballet dancers onstage. However, it is useful to remember that fashionable dress for women in the second two-thirds of the nineteenth century was also dominated by garments that confined the wearer's movements. During this period there was an evolution of styles in both fashion and stage wear, and costume design began to be taken seriously. Costume designers and makers alike gradually gained recognition until the twentieth century, when designers took all the credit and makers were relegated to small acknowledgments at the back of the theater program.

Throughout the nineteenth century, the number of theatrical costumiers working in major cities increased. Premier opera houses such as those in Paris and St. Petersburg had their own in-house costume ateliers, but as urban development exploded and theaters proliferated, commercial suppliers arose to accommodate them. Many began by supplying outfits for amateur productions and fancy-dress balls organized by society, forming a link between theater and fashion. By the end of the century, commercial costumiers based in London included Mons. & Mme Alias, Clarkson's, Miss Fisher, Samuel May, L and H Nathan, H & M Rayne, and John Simmons, all of whom advertised in the *Era Almanac*. Samuel May, of Covent Garden, advertised "Theatres, Public and Private, furnished with complete and accurate Costumes, on Sale or Hire." The ad also offered costumes for fancy-dress balls and the hire of court dress, and announced, "Managers producing Pantomimes can be supplied with good Second-hand Sets of Ballet and Pantomime Dresses." Rayne's supplied not only costumes but also wigs and hats, boots and shoes, tights, hosiery and "paddings." The latter were to ensure fashionably rounded figures—and legs! Alias and Miss Fisher supplied many of the ballet costumes.

The rise of costumiers paralleled the rise of fashion houses, some of which advertised their work by dressing celebrities, including performers, and supplying outfits to be worn onstage, but there appeared to be little crossover with dance costumes, which required special attention. It should be mentioned that the development of costume and fashion designers alike was aided by the invention of the sewing machine early in the century. The machines significantly speeded up the process, and the designers undoubtedly took advantage of new fabrics and the increased range of synthetic dyes—aniline violet, or mauveine, acid magenta, aldehyde green, Martius yellow, Magdala red—some of which may have been hazardous to the health.

Discussion of nineteenth-century costume for dance inevitably focuses on the development of the tutu. It is generally accepted that Eugène Lami, the in-house costume designer at the Paris Opera, originated the long, bell-skirted tutu for the 1832 Romantic ballet *La Sylphide*. As no design drawings survive, it may have been be an instance of taking a standard dance costume and creating a version in white that captured the audience's imagination. The Romantic tutu was gradually shortened to thigh length, as Italian ballet masters and ballerinas developed techniques such as balances on pointe and multiple turns that were hidden and/or hindered by the longer skirts. At the Paris Opera, however, where Italian technique was less in evidence, skirts generally remained longer. The leading British designer of ballet costumes at the end of the century, Wilhelm, described the tutu in the *Magazine of Art* (1895) as "an abbreviated perversion of a modern débutante's ball-dress, shorn of two-thirds of its length and décolleté to exaggeration."[1]

The only other element of ballet costume in the nineteenth century usually considered worthy of mention is the toe shoe. It was an adaptation of ladies' evening footwear—soft, straight slippers that could be worn on either foot. The ballet version was a delicate satin slipper with some additional stitching at the toe to support the foot. Marie Taglioni, the star of *La Sylphide*, apparently did not undertake turns on pointe and rose on pointe only briefly. But in the course of the century, the Italians stiffened the toe with hessian and

PRECEDING PAGES: François Gabriel Guillaume Lépaulle, portrait of Marie and Paul Taglioni in the ballet *La Sylphide*, 1832.

glue to make the block. This reinforced shoe assisted their advances in technique, and Italian ballerinas were frequently described as having pointes of steel. Although much emphasis is placed on the development of pointe work during the century, the corps de ballet in many popular productions wore only soft slippers or heeled shoes. As can be seen in surviving film footage of the *ballo grande* (spectacular ballet) *Excelsior*, the subject of which was progress in civilization and science,

many of the dancers did little more than rearrange their groupings and Wilhelm at the Empire in London sometimes regarded dancers as little more than "units of colour."[2]

Any discussion of links between nineteenth-century ballet costumes and fashion is handicapped by the dearth of extant costumes. The skirts of most tutus have disintegrated; generally, only the bodices or, as in the case of the great Marie Taglioni, the corselets and unblocked slippers have survived.

Black silk satin slippers, France, ca. 1835.

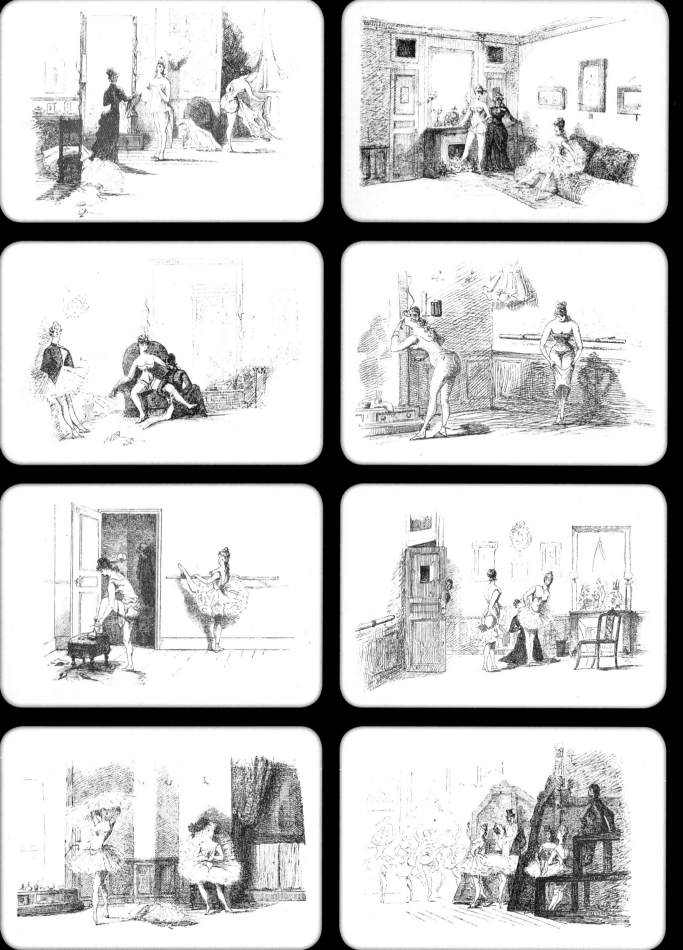

Although there are a number of extant late nineteenth-century tutus in St. Petersburg, analysis of the century's dance costumes relies heavily on period iconography. Illustrations, prints, and paintings infuse the costumes with life, whereas photographs tend to be static and unflattering, as dancers were forced to hold poses for the long exposures. There are also design sketches and written descriptions. Finally, the advent of film at the end of the century made it possible to view performances by star ballerinas and see costumes in movement.

Close inspection of the iconography of dancers' costumes reveals that over time there was considerable change in the shape of bodices and their necklines, in the shape of skirts, and in the way the dancers' hair was dressed, all of which may be linked to changes in fashionable dress, particularly evening wear. Fashion was not the only influence on ballet costume, however. There was also an abiding fascination with the classical worlds of Greece and Rome, prompting tunic-like costumes that allowed greater freedom of movement than costumes influenced by high fashion. Paintings, too, served as sources of costumes, and a growing interest in folk culture and customs, which led to a passion for national dress and archaeological exactness (at least in the nineteenth-century understanding of the term) influenced aspects of theatrical design. Nevertheless, wearing a tutu remained a badge of honor for a ballerina; in 1903, for instance, the dancer Héva Sarcy, who had just been given the lead role in the ballet in Massenet's opera *Hérodiade* at the Théâtre de la Gaîté, took the managers, the Isola brothers, to court when they insisted that she wear a floor-length "skirt of thick gauze," a "costume of a more historical cut and character." She was reported as saying, "No prima ballerina ever dances in anything but the short gauze petticoat called 'tutu.'"[5] Historical and long costumes were for character dancers and mimes. It "wounded her honour and the honour of her profession, . . . a ballet dancer had been given legs to show them."[4] Italian ballerinas Emma Palladino and Bettina de Sortis, then dancing at the Empire in London, were firmly of the school that considered tutus indispensable. "When she has learnt technical perfection, she likes to show that she possesses it, and that she cannot do in a long skirt."[5] Interestingly, in 1892 Pierina Legnani danced in long dresses for skirt dances and short tutus for her academic variations in *Don Juan* and *Aladdin* at the Alhambra in London.

Before tracing the development of the tutu, it seems appropriate to describe the undergarments dancers wore. They were cumbersome by modern standards yet reflect the underwear of contemporary dress. The dance historian Lillian Moore provided a detailed description of them in her account of rehearsal wear for dancers in the era of Degas's paintings: "First came a chemise, tied at the waist with a ribbon; then a little corset, laced up tight; then cotton panties and long cotton stockings fastened with suspenders; over these the ever-present bloomers; then a white batiste bodice, sleeveless, with a ruffle around the neck, and the double tarlatan skirts of the tutu. A neat sash around the waist completed the picture."[6] This dressing of a dancer is documented in a series of illustrations by A. Guillaumot fils for Maurice Magnier's 1885 book *La danseuse*. For performances, expensive tights were worn and the bloomers were replaced with more modest drawers. For additional modesty, layers of the underskirts of the tutu were sometimes stitched together, as, for example, in Copenhagen. But this practice hampered the ballerinas' ability to perform the Paris Opera tradition of finishing a solo with a *bouffante*, "a pirouette sur la pointe performed so that the skirt flared out to the delight of the gentlemen seated near the stage."[7] Tights became an essential garment for dancers, who were expected to provide them themselves. "A Ballet Girl" writing to *The Era* in 1877 noted that "tights, shoes and muslin dresses take over one pound to pay for out of our money."[8] In 1891 it was noted that worsted tights cost between 8 and 10 shillings and good silk tights between 30 and 40 shillings. Other dancers would stitch "pink sock stockings on to cotton tops of whitney-brown."

Dance costumes required as much craftsmanship as fashionable dress. Like high fashion, they were often lined and hand-finished, and incorporated strips of whalebone (baleen). The tutus' corsets and boned bodices dictated the movement of the dancer. The height of a dancer's arabesque was restricted by the boning, which would pinch the flesh as the hip made contact with the corset. By the 1880s, however, bodices that

Illustrations by A. Guillaumot fils for the book *La danseuse* by Maurice Magnier, 1885.

were heavily boned and laced like a corset were cut high on hips, allowing the leg to lift higher. To be more comfortable in their tight, restricting garments, the dancers held their bodies in a forward-tilting position. Throughout the nineteenth century, the range of body movement was limited and it was unusual for dancers to use their arms effectively. Given that they so often carried props, there was little opportunity to use their arms. Marie Taglioni was recognized as the rare dancer with a flexible torso. An anonymous author noted that under Taglioni's influence other dancers began to use "their arms and legs like ordinary mortals, they have even risked splitting their satin corsets by bending their bodies more."9

Rehearsal dress changed little in the last two-thirds of the century. The French writer Albéric Second described rehearsal attire in *Les Petits Mystères de l'Opéra* (1844):

> The girls are bare-headed and décolletées; their arms
> are bare, the waist confined in a tight bodice. A very
> short bouffant skirt, made of net or striped muslin
> reaches to the knees. Their thighs are chastely
> hidden under large calico bloomers impenetrable
> as a state secret. The men, without neck-ties, with
> bare throats, wear short vests of white material, and
> breeches reaching half way down the leg, fastening
> at the waist with a leather belt.

This description accords with the outfits that dancers in opera-house companies wore during rehearsals. The rank-and-file corps de ballet members of music hall productions dressed differently, as seen in a drawing by choreographer Carlo Coppi of a rehearsal at the Alhambra in London. Here, as described by Athol Mayhew, the dancers are "clad in a kind of demi-toilet" consisting of a lightweight, just-below-the-knee petticoat worn over white linen bloomers, with individual touches such as the colored "Garibaldi" and "black or fancy" stockings.10 The Garibaldi, originally a red wool shirt worn by supporters of the Italian patriot Giuseppe Garibaldi, became popular in the 1860s and was even worn by Empress Eugénie. Precursor of a woman's blouse, the Garibaldi was a comfortable garment with full sleeves. Rather than tucking it

into a skirt, the rehearsing dancers belted their Garibaldis and left the fabric hanging over the top of their petticoat-skirts. As seen in the drawing, most of the dancers wear low-heeled shoes, though one woman in a tutu-shaped skirt (who is possibly a coryphée, or soloist, rather than a corps de ballet member) wears soft slippers.

In 1981 British ballerina Alicia Markova wrote, "I often feel the greatest influence towards design came in the nineteenth century from two Frenchmen, Monsieur Maillot and Jules Leotard when they gave us tights and leotards which to this day have become the traditional clothes for dancers worldwide."11 Although more structured and lacking the elasticity of twentieth-century leotards, these body-hugging garments were often worn by women performing travesty roles. Sometimes they were worn with shorts, but at other times fabric would be draped over the hips. The leotard, or fitted jacket, plus the hip-draped style of costume echoed the fashion for decorative layering of fabric over dresses in the 1870s, minus the dresses' long full skirt! The costumes by Lucien Besche for the military ballet *Le Bivouac* (1885), reworked as *Our Army and Navy* (1889), show a range of designs for dancers in travesty roles. Cross-dressing proliferated at the end of the century; while male dancers performed character and virtuoso roles, the hero and the "men" in the corps de ballet were often played by women. Many "male" costumes featured long-skirted jackets, and costumes for up-to-date ballets (productions originating in music halls depicting contemporary scenes of life such as shopping and visits to the seaside) show women looking stylish in more fashionable men's attire.

In the first three decades of the nineteenth century, women's ballet costumes reflected the fashion for the Empire style, with the waist just under the bust and the skirt falling straight. These costumes, like Empire dresses, were often made in fine fabrics that were easy to move in. Thereafter, however, ballet costumes became more cumbersome. And, as the tutu evolved throughout the remainder of the century, the ballerina's appearance also changed. The fashionable wide, off-the-shoulder neckline of the mid-1830s and 1840s, evident in the bodices of the costumes worn by Fanny Elssler as Florinde in *Le Diable Boiteux* (1836) and Carlotta Grisi as

the title role in *Giselle* (1842) changed to the V-shaped neck-line of costumes in the 1870s, including those for Giuseppina Bozzacchi as Swanilda in *Coppelia*. The skirt shifted from the rounded "dome" to a "pyramidal" shape, usually joined to the bodice at the natural waist. Ballerinas' hairstyles also contributed to their fashionable appearance. In the 1840s Marie Taglioni's center-parted, smoothly looped-back hair reflected the look of the young Queen Victoria, whereas Pierina Legnani's curls piled high on her head in the 1890s echoed the style of Princess Alexandra of Denmark.

Even Marie Taglioni's *La Sylphide* costume evolved over the period during which she danced the role (1832–1847). In the earliest images, the costume had a rather loosely constructed bodice and straight skirt, and the cap sleeves had

a fullness they would lose. Over the course of the 1830s, the waistline of fashionable dress returned to its natural position and the décolleté bodice became low shouldered. By the 1840s, as clearly seen in *Souvenir d'adieu de Marie Taglioni* (1845), an album of prints after Alfred Edward Chalon's drawings. the costume featured a boned bodice cut to fit the natural waist at the sides and back and coming to a V in front, a configuration that enhanced the impression of slimness. The sleeves were tighter; the skirt, much fuller. The headdress was smaller, and Taglioni's hair was parted in the center with plaited oval loops at the sides (a hairstyle she would adopt offstage for the rest of her life). Though shorter, the shape of Taglioni's skirt bears a striking resemblance to that of the white dress Queen Victoria wore for her wedding in 1840.

Sir George Hayter, *The Marriage of Queen Victoria, 10 February 1840* (detail), 1840–42.

Another example of the link between dance costume and fashionable dress is seen in an 1849 lithograph of a drawing by the Danish designer Edvard Lehmann illustrating the divertissement *Pas des Trois Cousines* that August Bournonville choreographed for a production that premiered at the popular Casino Theatre in Copenhagen on May 20, 1848. The print depicts the performers, Sophie, Juliette, and Amalie Price of the English dance dynasty, dressed in costumes with wide, low-shouldered necklines and straight short sleeves. Their bodices are pleated in front, echoing the construction of contemporaneous high-fashion bodices, such as one dated ca. 1845 in The Museum at FIT's collection, on which the fabric has been gathered into pleats. The costumes' calf-length skirts are dome shaped, with the top layer caught up and ornamented, like the front of the bodices, with floral trimmings. The dancers' hair is parted in the center and looped round the ears.

Photographs of dancers who performed *Pas des Trois Cousines* in later years indicate that the costumes evolved in parallel with fashion. In an 1885 photograph of Charlotte Hansen, Elisabeth Soyer, and Eleonora Monti, the shoulders of the costumes are ornamented with bows and the necklines are decorated with lace. The bodices are fitted but have lost the pleated effect of the original, and the skirts are undecorated. A photograph taken two decades later (1905) shows the dancers wearing what the Danish ballet historian Knud Arne Jürgensen suggests is a "refined version of the obligatory school rehearsal dress," as by then the divertissement was danced only by students. The lace at the neckline is wider than in the past, and the conveniently raised arm of one of the dancers reveals tiny puffed sleeves underneath.

Photographs of dancers taken in the 1850s show voluminous skirts, probably consisting of a series of stiffened petticoats. It was the era of the crinoline; ballerinas obviously couldn't wear such caged constructions under their costumes, but the starched petticoats approximated the shape.[12] Skirt lengths were rising, but only to just below the knee, until the 1880s, when they were shortened considerably. Unlike the mini-skirt era of the 1960s and 1970s, the shorter skirts were not a reflection of a fashion trend but were undoubtedly the result of developments in ballet technique pioneered by Italian dancers. Such steps as the multiple fouetté turns perfected by dancers Maria Giuri and Pierina Legnani could not have been executed if they had been swathed in fabric. In 1885, when Virginia Zucchi was invited to dance Aspicia in *The Pharaoh's Daughter* at the Imperial Ballet in St. Petersburg, her tutu shocked some members of the audience for its transparency, low décolleté, and short skirt. On seeing the traditional tutu made for her by the theater, she asked for the skirt to be shortened but was told it was regulation length. On the day of the performance, proclaiming, "I will have my skirts short. I will not dance in a costume fit for a grandmother,"[13] she shortened the skirt to well above the knee. Soon thereafter, shorter skirts became accepted, as 1899 photographs of Russian ballerina Mathilde Kschessinska

OPPOSITE: Ivory silk gauze dress with shirred and smocked bodice, ca. 1845.
ABOVE: English performers Sophie, Juliette, and Amalie Price in *Pas des Trois Cousines,* choreography by August Bournonville, 1848.

performing the title role in *Esmeralda* indicate; the once long tutu is now extremely short.

During the 1880s and 1890s, tutus were fashioned with more fabric at the back to give them the effect of having a bustle. Whether the tutu was structured that way or extra ruffles were added to the back to an underskirt, as appears to be the case in images of some undressed dancers, is unclear.

The effect can be seen in photographs, including one of Legnani as Odette in *Swan Lake*, which would appear to be the source of a drawing on a program for the Apollo Theatre, Berlin, in the 1890s.

One production that indicated fashion's influence on costume was the influential "Snow Ballet" at the end of the third act of the *opéra féerie Le Voyage dans la lune*, first per-

Mariinsky Ballet corps de ballet members as Snowflakes in Marius Petipa's *The Nutcracker*, 1892.

formed at the Théâtre de la Gaîté, Paris, on October 26, 1875. According to the choreographer, Henri Justamant, he adapted the "Snow Ballet" from a ballet he had created for the Victoria Theatre, Berlin, in 1874, but it was Jacques Offenbach's score for *Le Voyage dans la lune* that made it such a success, spawning a flurry of snow ballets internationally. The only surviving vestige of this trend is the '"Waltz of the Snowflakes" in *The Nutcracker*. For all snow ballets, the white costumes were decorated with pom-pom snowflakes. The *Voyage dans la lune* snow costumes were designed by Alfred Grévin, and sketches and prints of his designs are tipped into Justamant's copy of the score, now in the Jerome Robbins Dance Collection at Lincoln Center. The costume sketch of the tutu features a white, thigh-length skirt and a fitted bodice with a hip-length basque, whereas an accompanying print indicates a longer, softer tulle underskirt. On the costume sketch, a thicker fabric decorated all over with white pom-poms is draped over one hip and caught up over the skirt. The print, in contrast, shows a longer, looped overskirt falling from the hips. The print has a row of bobbles at the top of the skirt and edging the low, straight-cut top. The bodice is decorated with a double row of white pom-poms, and there is double row at the neck. It is hard to detect straps, so an infill of flesh-colored fabric may have been used, and the costume may have had a high neck.

For the second London production of *Voyage dans la lune* at Her Majesty's Theatre in 1882, Wilhelm designed fuller, shorter tutus and was more restrained with the pom-poms. Photographs indicate that costume ideas for the corps de ballet in *The Nutcracker*'s snow scene incorporated many of the ideas. A caricature by the Legat brothers of O. Levenson as a snowflake shows that the Russian Imperial Ballet's costume for the snow scene in *The Nutcracker* retained the all-over decoration with pom-poms, a double row of pompoms at the top of the bodice, the hip-length basque, and the straight-cut bodice with narrow straps.

The "Snow Ballet" also featured a quartet of swallows, captured in Nadar's iconic photographs of the ballet. Grévin's original costume designs show that the shorts and bodice they wore over flesh-colored tights were red, and their winged

Kashmiri shawl woven with *buta* (floral motifs), draped over a cotton muslin gown, 1815–20.

jacket suggesting the bird was inky-colored. Wilhelm's 1882 design seems more successful than Grevin's, but both show the forward tilt of the body resulting from the corseting. Completing the costume is a fashionable red muff trimmed with white fur.

Ballets featured other fashionable accessories such as shawls. Kashmir shawls imported from India became popular in Britain in the late eighteenth century and in France from 1790 on. They were joined in the nineteenth century by embroidered silk shawls with fringe trim from China, which came to the West via Spain. Shawls and scarves were prominent accessories in many cultures, and they were often used in ballet to evoke associations with the classical world or the East. Shawls also played a dramatic role in ballets. In *La Sylphide*, the plaid shawl that James gives Effy is significant in act one, as is the shawl that Madge impregnates with poison in act two. Shawls, scarves, and ribbons are frequently used in nineteenth-century ballets to suggest architecture, extend movement, and decorate space. Pattern books for potential shapes survive, and the *pas de schall* became a cliché in many productions, but the effects it could achieve are hinted at by Frederick Ashton's use of ribbons in his *La Fille mal gardée.*

In the nineteenth century, there was more of a synergy between fashion and dance than a clear influence of one on the other. In the second half of the century, following the opening of trade with Japan and the profound impact that Japanese goods had at the Great International Exhibition in London in 1862, Japanese scenes began to be played out on the stage. The London exhibition included a booth in which Japanese artifacts collected by the British diplomat Rutherford Alcock were displayed, and the public was further fascinated by the delegation from Japan who visited wearing national dress. That event was followed by Japan's first official participation in the Exposition Universelle in Paris in 1867, where attendees had the opportunity to observe Japanese women smoking pipes in a tea store.

The fascination with Japan extended to adventurous women who took to wearing kimonos, largely in the privacy of their own homes. The actress Ellen Terry was photographed offstage in one. Beginning in the late 1860s, she was the partner of the artist-designer-architect Edward Goodwin, who was intrigued by Eastern arts. Onstage, kimonos most famously appeared in the Gilbert and Sullivan operetta *The Mikado* (1885), but they were also seen in ballets. Among the productions in which they were featured were *Yedda* (1879) and *Le Rêve* (1890) at the Paris Opera and *Yolande* (1877), *Oriella* (1991), and *In Japan* (1902) at the Alhambra in London. Whereas groups of dancers were dressed Japanese style, the ballerina was awkwardly costumed with a kimono over a tutu. A full set of the design tracings sent to a wardrobe for *In Japan* survive at Harvard, revealing the research that the designer, Comelli, undertook to re-create Japan onstage.

The point at which ballet and fashion really intersected was in late nineteenth-century up-to-date ballets. These were first danced in Britain in outer London music halls before being adopted by the Empire Theatre and subsequently the Alhambra, as well as other music halls in the city. Sports were often featured, including swimming, boating and cycling, providing an opportunity to show off the latest bathing suits, boating outfits, and bloomers worn for cycling.

Throughout the nineteenth century, the link between fashionable dress and ballet costume generally emerged in details of shape and decoration. But, as Taglioni's costume for *La Sylphide* shows, a single costume could change considerably over time to reflect developments in fashion. A costume from the later years that illustrates this evolution is Adeline Genée's for *The Dryad* (1906). When it premiered in Edwardian times, the costume featured heavy decoration on the front of the bodice and trailing scarves. But fashion quickly changed at the start of the twentieth century, and fashionable dress became straighter and generally simpler. Within a decade of the ballet's premiere, the Dryad's costume lost its sleeves and became a high-waisted tunic with only a cluster of violets and ivy for decoration, and the dancer wore her hair loose. By the early twentieth century and under the influence of costumes worn by Isadora Duncan and members of the Ballets Russes, the dancer returned to "the form of a woman as it is in Nature."

Silk taffeta morning robe with inserts of Japanese printed and embroidered crepe kimono fabric, ca. 1870.

Le Rêve costume illustrations by Alphonse Mucha, 1890.

TAGLIONI AND PAVLOVA: MAKINGS OF THE MODERN BALLERINA

PATRICIA MEARS

The resurgence of interest in classical ballet that swept Western Europe and America in the twentieth century constituted a modern infatuation with a very old art form. The technical foundation of ballet was created in the second half of the seventeenth century during the reign of Louis XIV, and the earliest works were performed almost exclusively by male members of the French aristocracy. Even though ballet moved from the court to the stage during the Baroque and Rococo eras, became professionalized, and included more women dancers, men remained its primary participants and overseers. After the French Revolution, however, ballet evolved into an increasingly urban and publicly accessible art form that came to be dominated by female professionals during the Romantic era of the 1830s and 1840s.

Before the rise of the Romantic ballerina, several pioneering eighteenth-century French dancers elevated ballet's technical, artistic, and aesthetic standards. One of the greatest was Marie Anne de Cupis de Camargo (1710–1770), or La Camargo, as she was called. Her brilliant *batterie* (rapid footwork) and *ballon* (buoyant jumps) were comparable to those of her male counterparts. To ensure that her superior technique would be visible, Camargo took the unprecedented step of raising the hemlines of her panniered skirts. This modification of a formal court costume for the ballet stage was outdone by Marie Sallé (1707–1756), Camargo's rival. For one performance, Sallé eschewed the corset and petticoat in favor of a muslin gown that she draped over her nearly naked body. Sallé's costume was meant to evoke the look of ancient Greek statuary, presaging by decades Neoclassicism, which would dominate art and design beginning at the end of the eighteenth century.

After the revolution, Paris replaced Versailles as the capital of France. It was on the city's stages that the greatest ballerina of her age, Marie Taglioni (1804–1884), led a technical and aesthetic revolution, introducing changes that survive to this day. Born into a family of dancers and entertainers, Taglioni became a star after her debuts in *The Ballet of the Nuns* in 1831 and *La Sylphide* in 1832. Rejecting regal Classicism in favor of a spiritual, supernal Romanticism, these ballets also featured the novelty of women dancing on *pointe*, or the tips of their toes, and a new costume with a diaphanous skirt that came to be known as the tutu. Taglioni, with her dark hair swept back into a low chignon, wore a décolletage-revealing, corseted bodice atop this new filmy and floaty "sylph" skirt, which fell just below the knee. Not only did Taglioni change ballet's style, but she also helped reposition the ballerina in society. More than any other dancer before her, she elevated ballet into a respectable art form in the 1830s and 1840s.

Several other factors contributed to ballerinas' social acceptability. Lithography, for one. Produced and disseminated throughout Europe, inexpensive but relatively high-quality lithographic prints of tutu-clad dancers resembling sylphs or fairies in mystical settings supplanted the perception of dancers as sexually available urban waifs.[1] These images were sometimes executed by the same hands who illustrated the latest fashion plates. A century later, the dancers and models depicted in French lithographs became vitally important sources of inspiration for both the ballet and the fashion communities, as the revival of Romanticism took hold.

Another factor were the enthusiastic writings of dance critics such as Jules Janin and Théophile Gautier. Thanks in part to their efforts, ballet became a woman's art form championed by men who celebrated not only the body in motion but also the body beneath the costume. It may seem a contradiction that men who exalted the sexuality of ballerinas could also advance their social position. The blend of beauty and talent, as exemplified by Fanny Elssler, a leading star of the era and Taglioni's chief rival, was especially appreciated. The critics did recognize and laud Taglioni's artistry, despite the fact that she was far from an ideal beauty. In fact, Taglioni was described as homely, even ugly, with thin, extra-long arms and a slightly hunched back. Nonetheless, she was ethereal and transcendent in performance.

A third, and perhaps more critical, factor was the support ballerinas received from female fans during the Romantic era. Again, much of the credit for this can be given to Marie Taglioni, who personified the ladylike image of the ballerina throughout Europe. Taglioni appealed to both men and women, the latter especially because she made such an effort to dress and deport herself like a proper lady, onstage

PRECEDING PAGES: Photograph of Anna Pavlova in *The Dying Swan*, 1905.
OPPOSITE: *Souvenir d'adieu de Marie Taglioni*, lithograph of Marie Taglioni in *La Sylphide*, 1845.

50

Lady Blessington concurred, noting that Taglioni received applause with "decent dignity" and eschewed the licentious style generally adopted by the ladies of her profession.

Even Queen Victoria was a fan. When she was still Princess Victoria of Kent, Taglioni was "as familiar a name in the royal household as that of any duke or general."[2] According to dance historian Caitlyn Lehmann, the princess was a regular visitor to the opera house and frequently recorded her impressions of Taglioni in her journal, appraising the ballerina's "inimitable" performances with the sincerity of a veteran.[3] The thirteen-year-old princess owned a Sylphide doll and later received "a very pretty print of Mdlle. [*sic*] Taglioni" for her sixteenth birthday. After winning a bet with the king at Ascot, Victoria was given a horse that Queen Adelaide christened Taglioni.

In addition to having dolls, children's costumes, and confections (Russian caramel candies and cakes) named in her honor, Taglioni may have been the first female ballet dancer to promote fashion trends. Images of the ballerina began to appear in fashion publications as early as 1830, before her debut in *The Ballet of the Nuns*. In one fashion plate, "Mlle. Taglioni, the Celebrated French Dancer" models the latest coiffeur. To her right is a woman dressed in an Italian folk costume and to her left, amazingly, is an image of Queen Adelaide, Victoria's aunt and wife of King William IV. If this identification is correct, the fashion press deemed Taglioni worthy of being positioned next to royalty.

Taglioni performed in London regularly and sparked, according to Lehmann, "a veritable bonanza for high-end retailers." For example, the English lady of fashion could avail herself of an array of textiles inspired by her greatest role: the "gauze sylphide," "tissu Sylphide" ("new and very pretty for walking bonnets"), "satin Sylphide" (described as "exceedingly soft and brilliant") and "rose-coloured mousseline Sylphide." Taglioni accessories were also available: an ivory-handled "La Sylphide" parasol and the "turban Sylphide" ("adapted to very youthful features").[4]

The ballerina also had an impact on fashion in other countries. Lodewijk Muns, a curator at the Nederlands Muziek Instituut, wrote a catalogue entry describing "bric à brac"

and off. Dressing in an attractive but simple way, Taglioni carefully crafted the image of herself as "an ideal bourgeois woman." Although her love life was rather salacious (she bore two children with men other than her husband and was the recipient of lavish gifts from wealthy lovers, including two palazzos in Venice and one on Lake Como), her costumes reflected her offstage tastes, as she accessorized her sylph tutus with discreet pearl bracelets and fresh floral diadems. According to Juliette Récamier, a leading Parisian socialite, Taglioni dressed like the middle- and upper-class ladies who came to see her dance—and they vied with the traditional all-male audience in numbers and enthusiasm. The Irish writer

ABOVE: Portrait of Marie Taglioni, ca. 1840. OPPOSITE: "Newest fashions for 1830," fashion plate featuring Marie Taglioni (center), 1830.

M.elle Taglioni,
the Celebrated French Dancer.

Queen Adelaide.   Newest Fashions for September 1830.   Costumes of All Nations. N.º 58.
Italian.

belonging to the ballerina. His research uncovered an entry from a German dictionary published in 1863. "*Taglionishawls*: Shawls named after Marie Taglioni; are made of wool, with a crossbar structure."[5]

The ballerina was associated with a number of corsets bearing her name or that of her most famous role. As Lehmann writes, "By 1835, there was Madame Saint Anton's 'Corset Perfectionne Sylphide,' promising 'perfect ease and comfort' and a 'sylph-like' figure for the wearer. Free from

steel and whalebone and 'precluding the necessity of tight lacing,' the corset was available from Madame's showrooms in London and Paris and was, so the advertisement ran, all the rage with the *haut ton*."[6] Fashion publications such as *Petit Courrier des Dames*, a leading magazine founded in France after the Napoleonic Wars, featured an image and description of Taglioni wearing a new corset.[7] Yet another publication, *Le Follet, Courrier des Salons, Journal des Modes*, featured an array of accessories and a "Taglioni corset with instant unlacing manufactured by Monsier Pousse, 28, rue Bourbon Villeneuve," dated 1837.[8]

Thanks to the continuing efforts of scholars, the range of fashionable looks and accessories connected to and possibly inspired by Taglioni is proving more expansive than previously thought, altering some assumptions that the ballerina had little if any influence on fashion. It is understood that the ballerina's white tutu and pointe shoes were modified versions of the high-fashion dress and footwear of the late 1820s–mid-1840s. But the corset Taglioni wore may have advanced and improved those that were commercially available to middle-class women. Softly constructed and exposing a good deal of the female form—specifically her neck, collar bone, upper back, and arms—Taglioni's corset was not inappropriately revealing. As Lehmann describes it, the ballet bodice mirrored the eveningwear that was worn by respectable women, and these women, in turn, embraced the Sylphide aesthetic.

No other ballerina attained Taglioni's combination of celebrity and respectability until the next century. There was one less accomplished dancer, however, who achieved great fame thanks to her self-promoting efforts: the ravishing demimondaine Cléo de Mérode. Born Cléopâtra Diane de Mérode in Paris in 1875, she was a classically trained dancer and made her professional debut at the age of eleven. She was more renowned, however, for her beauty, her tiny, tight-laced waist, and her rumored affair with King Leopold of Bavaria. Although the king's affairs with prostitutes supposedly tainted her reputation, de Mérode nonetheless became a trendsetting muse of artists, sculptors, and photographers, as well as an internationally recognized ballet dancer. At the peak of her fame, de Mérode chose to dance in a tutu at

Marie Taglioni corset in *Le Follet, Courrier des Salons, Journal des Modes*, December 3, 1830.

the Folies Bergère. Her performances caused a scandal and gained her even greater notoriety.

What made de Mérode so famous, even beyond the scandals and the stage, were photographic images of her that were widely distributed across Europe and beyond. Most of the images depict her in fashionable Belle Époque dresses and furs. But she was also photographed wearing tea gowns, historically inspired dress, and ballet costumes. The ballet costumes are especially provocative. She routinely donned very short, uncorseted tunics slit to the top of the hip and was photographed in shockingly short tutus, including a view from the back, a risqué ballet pose rarely seen before World War I.

The woman who did the most to elevate the status of classical dancers and reinvigorate the connection between fashion

Cléo de Mérode photographed in a tutu, from *Le Panorama: La danse, l'Opéra, le corps de ballet,* 1897.

and ballet was one of the art form's greatest ballerinas, Anna Pavlova. She is also credited with reviving and modernizing Taglioni-style Romanticism. Soon after Taglioni retired in 1847, the popularity of ballet began to wane in Paris. Though the dance form remained an integral part of French operas, it was in other countries such as Denmark that the Romantic style was perpetuated and advanced during the second half of the nineteenth century. And though Taglioni remained an important historical figure, a renewed interest in her style and aesthetic did not occur until the early twentieth century.

Pavlova played a major role in the Romantic revival that swept the ballet world, although the phenomenon reached its apogee after the ballerina's untimely death in 1931.

A super-thin, long-limbed, and subtly toned body dominates both fashion and ballet today, but tastes were vastly different in the latter part of the nineteenth century, when the Italian ballerinas Virginia Zucchi, Pierina Legnani, and Carlotta Brianza were dominant figures in Western Europe and Russia. These women have been described as plump and sturdy, with steely, muscular legs capable of astounding technical feats that sometimes (but not always, as some have reported) surpassed the abilities of their Russian counterparts. One of the most profoundly important aspects of Pavlova's artistry was that she made the lithe and delicate physique a modern standard in ballet.

Pavlova was born on February 12, 1881, in less than ideal circumstances. The illegitimate daughter of Lyubov Feodorovna, a laundress, and, as some speculate, the Russian Jewish banker Lazar Polyakov, she was named Anna Matveyevna Pavlova when her mother married Matvey Pavlov, who adopted her at the age of three. She saw her first ballet performance at the legendary Mariinsky Imperial Theater when she was eight, and she knew then that she wanted to be a dancer. But her small size and "sickly" appearance delayed her acceptance into the Imperial Ballet School in St. Petersburg by two years.

Pavlova's slim physique, perfectly shaped legs, and beautifully arched feet were noted even when she was a young girl. Although she was recognized as a prodigious talent by the time she graduated, and her look was widely emulated after she became famous, at first she had to overcome acute prejudices. Fellow ballerina Tamara Karsavina, a star of the Ballets Russes, noted in her memoirs that Pavlova "was so frail as to seem, in our opinion, much weaker . . . [U]ndiscerning admiration was all for virtuosity: our ideals shaped after a robust, compact figure of Legnani's type." Karsavina also noted that "Romanticism was not the fashion anymore. The very figure of our dancers, as compared with the silhouette of those a half century ago, clearly showed the reversion of taste . . . Meagreness being considered an enemy of good looks, the

Mariinsky Ballet prima ballerina Mathilde Kschessinska wearing an array of fine jewels, possibly by Fabergé, 1890s.

opinion prevailed that Anna Pavlova needed feeding up." But, wrote Karsavina, "Pavlova was destined to bring back to our stage the forgotten charm of the Romantic ballet of the days of Taglioni."[9]

Not only did Pavlova have to overcome the scorn of those who dismissed her delicate frame and less-than-perfect technique, but she also had to compete with a contemporary who dominated Imperial Russian ballet: Mathilde Kschessinska. Inspired by the Italians' technical skills and by Zucchi's dramatic gifts, Kschessinska epitomized high-style Russian glamour. Photographs of her in costumes as well as in a range of high-fashion garments, from fur coats to tea gowns, abounded.

The exchange and blurring between ballet costumes and real clothes was readily evident in Kschessinska's wardrobe. Not only was she the supreme dancer of her era (she was officially anointed prima ballerina), but she was also the mistress of the future Tsar Nicholas II and later became the wife of his cousin Grand Duke Andrei Vladimirovich. Her charm and allure were manifest in the material wealth she accumulated, including a grand home (which was taken over by Lenin after the 1917 Revolution) and a magnificent collection of jewels, which she wore on the Mariinsky stage. Diamonds and other gems were pinned in her hair and draped around her neck to dazzling effect. According to some sources, Kschessinska positively twinkled in her jewels, even while standing still.

In fact, it seems that outside of Russia, her jewels were almost as celebrated as the ballerina herself. Kschessinska rarely performed in the West. When she did, such as in her first Ballets Russes performance in London in the fall 1911 season, dancing the *Sleeping Beauty* pas de deux with Vaslav Nijinsky, her jewels earned much press. Kschessinska wrote in her autobiography that Sergei Diaghilev chose for her a "very beautiful blue costume, and together we discussed the question of the jewels I was to wear."[10] Newspapers detailed the ballerina's challenge of traveling with a treasury of expensive gems: the London branch of Fabergé, maker of many of her finest pieces, including a very expensive diadem, stored her cache and also procured a professional security detail while she danced and attended social functions.

Kschessinska created the template for the ultimate ballerina during the waning days of the Russian Empire. Although she is less well remembered than Pavlova, her obsessive focus on costume, jewels, and fashion amplified her persona and enhanced her validity as a grand dame of both the stage and society. Kschessinska was a wealthy, well-connected woman with many aristocratic friends, and she dressed accordingly. Her richly ornamented clothes and jeweled head were requisite elements in her world. And her costumes, likewise ornamented, would become standard elements of lavish ballet productions, especially those featuring royal and aristocratic characters.

In matters of style, Pavlova may have taken her inspiration from Kschessinska. She did not have an armory of jewels, but she was always fashionably dressed. As a ballerina, she performed tirelessly for two decades around the world, and photographs of her were just as widely disseminated. Pavlova crafted the ideal of the delicate and winsome, but also soulful and dramatic, ballerina, as well as the public's belief that ballerinas were mirrors of fashion.

In his photo-filled biography of Pavlova, published in 1982, author Keith Money devotes two short chapters to her fashions. The first presents a dozen images dating from 1908 to 1914.[11] As Money notes, the array of clothing—day suits, cloaks, tea gowns, and eveningwear—was beautifully modeled by Pavlova and worn with few adornments like jewelry. The one exception was her penchant for large, boldly festooned headwear, as was the fashion of the day. Though Pavlova reportedly was a patron of a number of couture houses, only a few garments can clearly be identified as coming from Mariano Fortuny, the Spanish artist-turned-textile-and-clothing designer, and Liberty of London. Some of her neoclassical-style gowns look very much like the work of Paul Poiret or Lucile.

The simplicity she preferred continued through the next phase of her sartorial life. Money documents her fashions in fourteen images dating from 1920 to 1927. He states that Pavlova altered some of her earlier garments in the mid-1920s, shortening them as fashionable skirt lengths rose to just below the knee.

For all her interest in fashion, Pavlova did not chart or set trends per se. Rather, she insured that every image of her, whether in a tutu or in streetwear, was exacting in portraying her as a beacon of style. Managing and controlling her persona was integral to defining the legend of the great ballerina. And, like her artistic predecessor Marie Taglioni, Pavlova laid the groundwork for the next generation of dancers, who would embrace and eventually reshape fashion.

Beyond her image, Pavlova's artistry changed the trajectory of classical ballet. Just as the Ballets Russes inspired an entire generation to take up the profession, so did the ballerina. Her performances may have been more traditional—singularly focused around her dancing—and her company of dancers less technically expert than Diaghilev's, yet Pavlova nonetheless redirected the course of modern ballet. Not only did she have legions of enamored fans, but she also trained young British girls at her London manse, Ivy House. They went from being her pupils to members of her traveling company, and, eventually, they spread ballet throughout Britain.

No Pavlova convert, however, was more important to ballet in the West than the dancer and choreographer Frederick Ashton. On the first page of Julie Kavanagh's biography of him, Ashton describes the impact that Pavlova's performance in Lima, Peru, had on him. The son of British expats in South America, the then thirteen-year-old decided, after a disappointing first impression, that she was the "greatest theatrical genius he had ever seen." Despite her rather garish stage makeup and her less-than-perfect technique, he noted that she "was a sprite, a flame" and that she "wasn't human. . . . Seeing her at that stage was the end of me. She injected me with her poison and from the end of that evening I wanted to dance."[12]

Dance specialists have observed that Pavlova loomed large over Ashton for the rest of his long life. His future muse, Margot Fonteyn, was one of numerous ballerinas who danced his works in the shadow of Pavlova's influence. Toward the end of her life, Fonteyn remarked that she "always felt that Fred was seeing Pavlova"[13] and that she was unable to meet his vision of the Russian legend. But it was Fonteyn who carried classical ballet forward on her similarly svelte, couture-clad frame.

ABOVE: Anna Pavlova in a silk "Delphos" tea gown by Mariano Fortuny, Berlin, ca. 1914.
OPPOSITE: Red pleated-silk "Delphos" gown with glass beads and silk cord by Mariano Fortuny, ca. 1920.

OPPOSITE: Portrait of Anna Pavlova, ca. 1912.

ABOVE: Georges Lepape, *Les Choses de Paul Poiret vues par Georges Lepape*, "Dame et perroquet," pochoir print, 1911.

BALLET AND COUTURE IN THE MID-CENTURY

PATRICIA MEARS

At the time of the Ballets Russes' debut in Paris in 1909, it is doubtful that anyone could have predicted that London would become the nexus of classical ballet outside of Russia, to be rivaled only by New York City. Yet ballet was the art form that connected artists and intellectuals across multiple disciplines, simultaneously inspiring a whole generation of young girls from the working and middle classes to take up dancing. Because ballet intertwined high culture and working-class aspirations, it should not be surprising that it also began to influence fashion.

English ballet was heavily indebted to the Ballets Russes. Though the company's hallmark modern works were inspirational, it was their full-length production of the Imperial Russian masterpiece *The Sleeping Beauty* that proved most influential. Arguably the greatest of the classical ballets, *The Sleeping Princess* (as Diaghilev called it) was set to what critics believe is Tchaikovsky's finest score. The original production by the legendary Mariinsky Ballet debuted in St. Petersburg in 1890, and it was responsible for converting the young Sergei Diaghilev to classical dance. His 1921 London production of *Beauty* was not the blockbuster hit he hoped for, but it became "the foundation of British ballet culture, which for many people in the West … was ballet culture itself."[1] *Beauty* later became the signature work of that nation's leading dance company, the Royal Ballet, and its most celebrated ballerina, Margot Fonteyn.

Diaghilev boasted of his own prescience. He noted: "I was always ahead of my time . . . but this time too many years." *The Sleeping Princess*'s success and long-term impact were a bit slow to gain traction, yet the impresario knew he was laying the groundwork for a great shift in ballet's future. During the interwar years, radical modernism gave way to the rise of historicism. Thanks in large part to the fervor of British talents who were profoundly influenced by the 1921 production of *Beauty*—mainly Ninette de Valois, Marie Rambert, and Frederick Ashton, all former Ballets Russes dancers—classical ballet would awaken and thrive on the stages of London.

It is an irony that "toe dancing," once viewed as a tawdry form of entertainment in Great Britain, became that nation's most beloved and popular performing art beginning around 1930. Against all odds, the Royal Ballet (originally called the Vic-Wells Ballet and later the Sadler's Wells Ballet) was born and thrived during one of the most difficult periods in modern history—the worldwide Depression of the 1930s, World War II, the onset of the Cold War in the late 1940s, and the rebuilding of Europe in the 1950s.

Much of the credit for Britain's ballet genesis goes to Dame Ninette de Valois (1898–2001). Born Edris Stannus in Ireland, she was a Ballets Russes alumna who went on to found the Royal Ballet and its school, as well as the Birmingham Royal Ballet, thus earning the nickname "godmother" of English ballet. Aside from forming and leading these entities for decades, as well as grooming both Ashton and Fonteyn, she canonized a small number of full-length Russian works dating to the late nineteenth century that would become the modern incarnation of "classical" ballet.

Ninette de Valois's efforts were supported by an emerging group of British balletomanes, as they called themselves: Philip Richardson, Cyril Beaumont, Arnold Haskell, and especially the renowned economist John Maynard Keynes. (Keynes was so impassioned a fan that he, although homosexual, married ballerina Lydia Lopokova in 1925.) During and shortly after World War II, Keynes was a member of the Council for the Encouragement of Music and the Arts (CEMA) and was instrumental in securing government funds for the Sadler's Wells Ballet and Covent Garden Opera House. Although Sadler's Wells regularly commissioned and performed one-act ballets like its precursor, the Ballets Russes, it was the revival of full-length classics—*Giselle*, *Swan Lake*, and especially *The Sleeping Beauty*—that became the company's hallmarks.

The British presentations of these classics were still a few years off when Frederick Ashton, that nation's greatest choreographer, debuted his first ballet on June 15, 1926, entitled *A Tragedy of Fashion, or The Scarlet Scissors*. Featuring Marie Rambert and Ashton himself in the leading roles, it is the story of a couturier, Monsieur Duchic, who commits suicide after his latest fashion collection is poorly received. The ballet was actually a lighthearted work and was full of fashion and ballet references. The *Maitresse de Maison* was named

Orchidée, and the house models were called Désir du Cygne (swan's desire) and Rose d'Ispahan. The clients are named Viscount and Vicountess Viscosa (after the synthetic fiber viscose, produced by the wealthy industrialist, art collector, and balletomane Samuel Courtauld). In addition to the title, setting, and story line, the characters Orchidée and Désir were inspired by fashion women in Ashton's social circle: Dorothy "Dody" Todd, the fiercely talented editor in chief of British *Vogue*, and her partner, Madge Garland, who was also an edi-

tor at the magazine. Todd was credited with elevating *Vogue*'s intellectual content; she increased the magazine's coverage of literature and the arts, including ballet.

Ashton's ballet expressed other connections between dance and fashion. He was inspired by two Ballets Russes productions choreographed by Bronislava Nijinska: *Les Biches* (The Does, French slang for young beauties) and *Le Train Bleu*. Depicting a summer party and travel to the South of France, respectively, the ballets were snapshots of the rather

Marie Rambert (center), Frederick Ashton, and Frances James (right) in Ashton's *A Tragedy of Fashion, or The Scarlet Scissors*, London, 1926.

frenetic pursuit of the leisurely lifestyle enjoyed during the Roaring Twenties. Garland encouraged Ashton's interest in fashion; perhaps this emboldened the choreographer to suggest that Coco Chanel design the costumes. Rambert flatly refused. Not only could they not afford the couturière, but Rambert also correctly understood that clothing is not costume. In fact, Rambert felt that Diaghilev's one mistake was choosing Chanel as the costume designer for *Le Train Bleu*.[2] Instead, professional costumier Sophie Fedorovich was hired, and she and Ashton became lifelong friends and collaborators.

There are two other minor fashion notes related to *A Tragedy of Fashion*. One is that a dancer in the original production was Frances James, sister of couturier Charles

James. The other is that a sculpture depicting a scene from the ballet is now part of the Victoria & Albert Museum's permanent collection. It was created on the fiftieth anniversary of the work in 1976 by the artist Astrid Zydower (1930–2005) and donated by Rambert to an institution with one of the world's great fashion and theater collections. This interaction among artists of all disciplines, intellectuals, and members of high society was crucial in laying the groundwork for the creation of British ballet by Brits.

Modern ballets continued to dominate the Ballets Russes' programming during the 1920s. However, the impact of *The Sleeping Princess* and a small but potent selection of Romantic-style works by the company's leading choreog-

Ballets Russes prima ballerina Tamara Karsavina as Columbine in Michel Fokine's *Carnaval*, June 1919.

rapher, Michel Fokine, was a harbinger of the classical and romantic wave that later came to define mid-twentieth-century ballet. Likewise, a small contingent of couturiers—mainly Jeanne Lanvin and the Boué Soeurs (sisters)—designed a range of romantic and full-skirted dresses that were successful alternatives to the sleek *moderne* sheaths and tunics.

One homage to the Romantic-style ballet was Fokine's 1909 one-act ballet *Les Sylphides*, set to the orchestrated version of Fredrick Chopin's piano works (the ballet was originally called *Chopiniana*), replete with long, sylph-style tutus. The costumes were nearly identical to those of the new Ballets Russes production of the 1841 classic, *Giselle*, which premiered in Paris in 1910. That year also saw the debut of another full-blown Romantic-style work by Fokine titled *Carnaval*. Set to music by Robert Schumann, with sets and costumes by Léon Bakst, it starred Tamara Karsavina as Columbine. The ballerina wore a white, full-skirted dress with tiers of scalloped ruffles ornamented with large dots. While the costume presaged the dominant fashion silhouette of the World War I era, it may also have inspired a specific garment designed by couturière Jeanne Lanvin. For her winter 1924–25 collection, Lanvin created an ivory silk taffeta gown in the *robe de style de dixhuitième siècle* (eighteenth-century-style dress) with black velvet circles appliquéd on the skirt and a red silk velvet bow around the waist. Is it a coincidence that Lanvin named it "Columbine"?

Interestingly, Lanvin's *robe de style* (as it is popularly known), with its dropped waist and billowing, flared skirt, was also called the "Camargo" frock, after the Rococo-era ballet dancer Marie Camargo, who was famous for shortening her panniered gowns to reveal her virtuoso footwork. Such dresses were not only evocative of *Carnaval*, but they also echoed the Rococo-style costume worn by the Lilac Fairy in the 1921 *Sleeping Princess*.

Jeanne Lanvin was a facile creator whom Karl Lagerfeld praised as a "great, great designer."[5] During her heyday in the 1920s, she designed everything, including menswear, children's clothing, accessories, and furs, in addition to a full range of women's fashions, from slim sheaths to her full-skirted *robes de style*, ornamented with the most exquisite embroi-

dery. During the interwar years, she produced numerous designs with reflective, circular elements made from materials such as metallic lamé, sequins, and mother-of-pearl. In the same season as her black-and-white "Columbine" dress, she created a version made of pale, yellow-green silk taffeta ornamented with silver lamé circles rimmed with white pearls and finished with a black bow instead of a red one.

There is evidence that Lanvin was directly involved with classical ballet in 1924. Dance historian Lynn Garafola discovered a cache of letters written by Russian-born ballerina Lydia Lopokova to her husband, John Maynard Keynes, in the archives of King's College, Cambridge University. Among

"Columbine" *robe de style* evening dress by Jeanne Lanvin, winter 1924–25. *Vogue*, December 1, 1924.

ABOVE: Pochoir print of dancer Ida Rubenstein in *La Dame aux Camélias*, dress by Worth. *Gazette du Bon Ton*, no. 5, 1923.
OPPOSITE: Pochoir print of dancer and actress Paulette Duval, dress by Georges Doeuillet. *Gazette du Bon Ton*, no. 1, January/February 1920.

the letters was a group that documented the creation of a small dance troupe comprised of world-class choreographers, dancers, and designers. Conceived by Comte Étienne de Beaumont, this company, Les Soirées de Paris, "aspired to replace the Russian Ballet [Ballets Russes] as the vanguard of the Paris artistic world," but it "has remained no more than a footnote to the dance history of the twenties."[4]

Despite the company's less-than-stellar impact, it performed more than half a dozen works in the spring of 1924. Among them was *Vogue*. Based on a poem by the fashionable novelist Paul Morand, the story, described as "three danced pages," is a love triangle set on the Lido beach. Lopokova mentions being "dressed by the couturière Lanvin." She does not describe the shape of the dress but notes that it was "made up of miroirs [mirrors] (dernier cri naturally)."[5] As the couturière used small, mirrored discs with some regularity at the time, a viable guess can be made as to what the ornamentation looked like.

Lanvin was a decidedly romantic designer, so it is no surprise that she consistently produced garments in this style. But Romantic ballet's impact must have been strong enough in the 1920s to inspire the avowed modernist Madeleine Vionnet. One of the twentieth century's greatest couturiers, Vionnet hand-draped each of her original designs and, in the process, elevated the craft of dressmaking to an art form. By abandoning the traditional practice of tailoring body-fitted fashions composed of numerous, complex pattern pieces and minimizing the cutting of fabric, Vionnet combined her study of classical and non-Western dress with her masterful dressmaking skill and her uncanny understanding of planar, or Euclidean, geometry to create new forms of construction. There is no evidence that she was a ballet fan. However, the couturière claimed that she was inspired by *the* modern dance pioneer, Isadora Duncan, as kinetic movement was an integral element of Vionnet's visually spare but physically dynamic crepe dresses.

Many couturiers embraced the Romantic ballerina aesthetic beginning around 1934, but Vionnet began to experiment with the idea a decade earlier. For example, at the 1924 Salon d'Automne design fair in Paris (November 1–December

Silk satin and muslin evening dress with "ballerina" skirt by Madeleine Vionnet, Paris, 1924.

14), one installation, designed by René Herbst for the man-nequin manufacturer Siegel, featured three Vionnet designs from her autumn/winter 1924–25 collection. Among them was an evening dress called "Ballerina"; a period photograph indicates that the bodice was made of silk velvet and the skirt of tulle godets. The dress was not only photographed in situ at the exposition but was also illustrated by the Italian Futurist Thayaht for the luxury fashion publication *La Gazette du Bon Ton*. Printed in the stencil-based pochoir style, the two-page spread depicted the "Ballerina" gown among Vionnet's more typical, streamlined designs.

This interplay between the *moderne* and the Romantic ballerina aesthetic in the 1920s was also evident in the look of some fashion models. Leading professionals incorporated ele-ments of the dancer's aesthetic. Among the best of them was Marion Morehouse, wife of the poet e.e. cummings. Although taller and less physically fit than a typical ballerina, she was nonetheless lean and elegant, with dark features that were as soulful as they were haughty. Her dark, glossy hair, pulled back into a ballerina-style chignon, heightened this effect.

This modern connection between fashion and the balle-rina was further exemplified by the appearance of dancers in

"À Biarritz, chez Madeleine Vionnet," pochoir print of Vionnet's "Ballerina" dress by Thayaht. *La Gazette du Bon Ton*, 1924–25.

leading fashion magazines, especially as models, beginning in the 1920s. The March 1, 1924, issue of *Vogue*, for instance, featured two images of the American ballerina Desiree Lubowska, photographed by Edward Steichen in two couture garments, one by Lanvin and the other by the leading New York retail and design house, Henri Bendel. Born Winnefred Foote in Faribault, Minnesota, in 1893, she not only adopted a Russian name (a common practice among Western dancers during the interwar period) but also spoke with an accent and falsely claimed to have Russian dance training. In addition to forming the short-lived National American Ballet Company in 1921 and having a brief career on Broadway and in film, Lubowska became involved with the fashion world. In 1921 she danced at the International Silk Exposition in New York, where, embodying the "Spirit of Silk," she burst forth from a cocoon. She also danced at the annual meetings of the National Garment Retailers' Association and the New York League of Advertising Women. Lubowska apparently carefully controlled her image: she sued the perfume and talcum powder company V. Vivaudou for using an unauthorized photo of her "in scant attire" in a newspaper advertisement.[6]

Though she has been forgotten over time, Lubowska received a great deal of press during her career. And she clearly was viewed as sufficiently stylish and elegant to find her way onto the pages of *Vogue*. Long and lean, with patrician features, her image was similar to that of both Marion Morehouse and the tall, long-limbed Ballets Russes ballerina Felia Doubrovska. Collectively, they advanced the idea of the ballerina as fashion paragon.

By the early 1930s and throughout World War II, the ballerina was a fashion magazine mainstay. Nearly every other issue of *Vogue* and *Harper's Bazaar* included ballet references and imagery. Editorials regularly featured news about the sets and costumes of new works, advertisements with ballet allusions, and photographs of ballerinas wearing both the latest fashions and costumes. What is interesting to note is whom the magazines chose as models, because the quality of their artistry was not the only criterion for their prominence in fashion publications. An examination of the array of dancers who appeared on the pages of fashion magazines makes the

OPPOSITE: Model Marion Morehouse wearing an evening dress by Lucien Lelong. *Vogue,* October 15, 1925.
ABOVE: American ballet dancer Desiree Lubowska. *Vogue,* March 1, 1924.

Balanchine sought fresh, emerging talents who could master and advance his increasingly challenging choreography and fulfill his modernist aesthetic, which eventually brushed away any vestige of the whalebone-corseted ballerina of the nineteenth century. As an added benefit for fashion, each girl was beautiful, especially Toumanova. Of part Georgian descent, she carried on the tradition of the pale-complexioned, dark-featured Russian ballerina à la Pavlova. In the *Vogue* editorial, photographer George Hoyningen-Huene astutely captured her in a wistful pose, with her pale tulle *Cotillon* costume billowing around her.

Fashion editors must have adored Toumanova and Baronova. Though Toumanova garnered the earlier press, Baronova began to be featured in the fashion magazines with increasing regularity in the late 1930s. As a dancer with the Ballet Russe de Monte Carlo, which was based in the United States during World War II, Baronova likely had ready access to fashion photographers, many of whom were based in New York City. (The Ballet Russe had a grueling travel schedule that took them across North and South America for months at a time. When not on tour, most of the dancers settled in and around the Big Apple.) Although fair-haired and more voluptuous than her colleagues, Baronova was both compelling on stage and beautiful in photographs.

Perhaps the most surprising ballerina model of the era was another member of the Ballet Russe de Monte Carlo, Sono Osato (1919–2018). A number of dancers interviewed for this book who knew Osato attest to the fact that she was exceptionally gorgeous. Though a good dancer, she was not considered an artist for the ages. Her inherent physical attributes may explain how someone of part Japanese descent became one of the most frequently featured ballerina models in the United Stated during World War II. While her Japanese-born father was shipped off to an internment camp, and she was denied a visa to travel with the Ballet Russe to Mexico, Osato maintained a constant presence in *Vogue* and *Harper's Bazaar*.

For a decade, from 1938 to 1948, Osato modeled lingerie, activewear, and evening gowns. Images of her in rehearsal and on the stage were also featured. What made her so desir-

preferences clear: ballerina models needed to be physically *and* facially beautiful. A beautiful face, though advantageous, was not crucial to a dancer's success on stage, but it was essential in fashion imagery.

The 1932 issue of *Vogue* mentioned in the Introduction featured images of the Ballet Russe de Monte Carlo's production of *Cotillon*, choreographed by George Balanchine. Its star was thirteen-year-old Tamara Toumanova. She was one of a lithe trio of youngsters recruited by Balanchine that season. The others were another thirteen-year-old, Irina Baronova, and fifteen-year-old Tatiana Riabouchinska. The daughters of Russian émigrés, their virtuosity and precocity prompted the inevitable sobriquet "baby ballerinas."

"New Russian Ballet," featuring Tamara Toumanova in George Balanchine's *Cotillon*, costume by Christian Bérard. *Vogue*, September 15, 1932.

Ballet Russe de Monte Carlo dancer Sono Osato in a Jo Pattullo gown. *Harper's Bazaar*, September 15, 1941.

able were not only her exquisite face and toned body but also her ability to move and improvise as well as, if not better than, a professional model. In an interview with Osato in 2017, she confirmed that for a 1938 fashion editorial, she serendipitously created a headpiece out of a necklace.[7] *Harper's Bazaar* noted, "Miss Sono Osato, the beautiful Japanese-American dancer of the Ballet Russe, wearing Chanel's liquid bowknot of rhinestones, with the bow lying flat and the pendants dripping over her forehead like a fringe of dewdrops."[8] This spontaneous self-adornment may have been encouraged by the photographer, George Platt Lynes. He was able to capture the connection between dance and fashion better than any photographer of his time, and his work often included

daring and provocative images of dancers, both male and female, in which the nude body is glorified.

Osato also disclosed that the magazine editors sought her out and that she made no conscious effort to find work as a model. She noted that she was not paid for her fashion work, or at least was not well compensated. Osato's recollections indicate that there must have been an awareness of ballet among members of the fashion community. Furthermore, her Japanese ancestry had little if any adverse effect on her fashion-related activities. It should be remembered that *Vogue* and *Harper's Bazaar* were widely read publications and were considered the bibles of high fashion in American. A beautiful dancer trumped racism even at the height of the war in the Pacific.

Osato was not the only dancer of mixed race or nationality to find her way into fashion publications. The Danish-Indonesian ballerina Nini Theilade also appeared in editorials. And others, such as the Jewish-Irish star Alicia Markova (born Alice Marks in London), were regulars in fashion publications. Markova's story was one of the great events of modern ballet history. Dubbed the "child Pavlova," she was a remarkably gifted dancer who was handpicked by Diaghilev himself to join the Ballets Russes in 1925, when she was only fourteen years old. She was also the first great British-born ballerina.

Markova's technique and artistry were perfectly balanced; her dancing was described as ethereal and transcendent. Likewise, her physique was ideally suited to the Romantic roles at which she excelled. Her face, however, was not, at least not for fashion. It is true that Markova was featured in numerous editorials, both in costume and in an array of high-style ensembles. But the frequency of her appearances in fashion magazines did not equal the brilliance of her dancing, and she was sometimes passed over for magazine shoots in favor of lesser talents. Also, a number of Markova photographs hide her face or display only her feet.

Markova's biographer, Tina Sutton, effectively argued that one of the reasons the ballerina was marginalized by the fashion magazines was the fact that she was Jewish. (The dancer's prominent "Jewish" nose was cited as a drawback. To her credit, Markova was decidedly proud of her heritage

ABOVE AND OPPOSITE: Ballet Russe de Monte Carlo dancer Sono Osato wearing a Coco Chanel necklace as a headpiece and modeling a Lucien Lelong gown. *Harper's Bazaar*, May 1938.

and never underwent cosmetic surgery to alter her appearance, as numerous other ballerinas did.) For example, Sutton concluded that anti-Semitism was the reason that Margot Fonteyn was awarded the supreme title of prima ballerina assoluta, as well as a DBE, before Markova, even though Markova was older and a firmly established star long before Fonteyn was. There is no doubt that anti-Semitism existed and played a role, but what the biographer did not take into account is the fact that the timing of Markova's career did not coincide with the heyday of Great Britain's greatest dance company. Markova was a pioneer and a freelance star who danced around the world with an array of companies while Fonteyn was the uncontested star of the Sadler's Wells Ballet and became its ideal representative. Furthermore, Fonteyn remained in Great Britain throughout the war, dancing on any stage and under any conditions as the Nazis bombed the island nation relentlessly, while Markova had settled in the United States. Fonteyn was rewarded for her patriotism by ardent British fans.

Throughout the 1930s and for the next several decades, ballet's ranks became increasingly diverse, as dancers from Russia and Western Europe were joined by those from both North and South America. Spanning eleven time zones, the Soviet Union alone produced a wide array of dancers, from Slavs (Russians, Belorussians, Ukrainians) to Georgians, Armenians, Baltic peoples, Turkic Muslims, Tatars, and Jews.

The roster of British dancers was also quite diverse, including those of English, Scottish, Irish, Jewish, and Brazilian backgrounds. And they hailed from the farthest reaches of the British Empire, moving to London from places as distant as Australia and South Africa. Even the most British of dancers, Margot Fonteyn, was of mixed ethnicity. She inherited her dark hair and features and her olive complexion from her Brazilian grandfather, Antonino Gonçalves Fontes. A world-traveling businessman, he had an affair with a young, unmarried Irish woman named Evelyn Acheson, Fonteyn's maternal grandmother. The ballerina's Brazilian roots were not immediately apparent, as she was born Margaret "Peggy" Hookman. But the fact that she changed her name to one that closely resembled her maternal grandfather's

and that she married a Panamanian diplomat, Tito Arias, attests to Fonteyn's affinity for her Latin American ethnicity. Furthermore, when her engineer father relocated the family to Shanghai during the 1920s, her straight, dark hair cut in a pageboy and her almond-shaped eyes earned her the moniker "the Chinese girl" from her classmates. Fonteyn's dark coloring and features à la Pavlova may have been one of the reasons why Ninette de Valois handpicked and groomed her for greatness. It was de Valois who first cast Fonteyn in starring roles when she was just seventeen, then kept her name and presence at the top of the company's roster for decades.

At the same time in America, the range of ethnicities was perhaps the broadest, as ballerinas of Asian, African, Latin American, and even American Indian descent populated the ranks of emerging companies as well as the Ballet Russe de Monte Carlo, which was stranded in the United States during World War II. The Eurasians mentioned earlier, Sono Osato and Nini Theilade, shared the stage and ballet classes with Jews Nora Kaye and Melissa Hayden; American Indians Rosella Hightower, Moscelyne Larkin, Yvette Chouteau, Marjorie Tallchief, and her older sister, prima ballerina Maria Tallchief; Latinas Alicia Alonso of Cuba and Lupe Serrano of Mexico; and African Americans Janet Collins and Raven Wilkinson. It should be noted that many black dancers were denied access to training and suffered more strident racial prejudice during their careers. It was not until Arthur Mitchell, the first black principal dancer in New York City Ballet, formed Dance Theater of Harlem in 1969 that more African Americans were able to make classical ballet a career.

This international, multicultural assemblage of talent was not, however, equally reflected in fashion. Though ballet was overwhelmingly populated by Europeans, it was just progressive enough to include those of different backgrounds. By comparison, fashion publications did not feature non-white models until the 1960s.

Ballet's impact on fashion was firmly in place by 1934: ballerinas had begun modeling; couturiers were adapting elements of stage costumes in their designs; and romanticism was becoming a fashion mainstay. Ballet had taken root in Britain and was on the cusp of becoming a major cultural movement. And it was still a creative force in France. Paris had been greatly influenced by the Ballets Russes and the influx of talent that fled Russia after the 1917 Revolution. Aside from dancers, choreographers, composers, artists, and critics, teachers trained at the Mariinsky were instrumental in maintaining Paris's importance as a ballet center. By the 1930s, retired émigré ballerinas such as Olga Preobrajenskaya were running renowned studios that attracted dancers from around the world.

But the modernism and exoticism of the Ballets Russes began to fall out of favor by the onset of the Depression, and historicism—initially neoclassicism and later neo-romanticism—took hold. Fashion designers on both sides of the English Channel began incorporating elements of the neo-romantic ballet costume: yards of tulle for long, full skirts and fitted bodices that were either paired with billowy sleeves or swathed in shawls made from transparent fabrics. Even pioneers of the modernist aesthetic such as Madeleine Vionnet and Coco Chanel started producing gowns with skirts that wafted like the sylph-style tutus of old, though theirs were more varied in color. When their designs were photographed for fashion magazines, the captions sometimes alluded to ballet. One Vionnet creation made of pink tulle and silver lamé was described as a "dress for [Vera] Zorina to dance in."[9]

As noted earlier, certain key ballets such as *Cotillon* had a direct influence on fashion. The sets and costumes for *Cotillon* were both designed by the French artist Christian Bérard and executed by Russian-born Barbara Karinska, a costumier who would later gain renown as chief costume designer for the New York City Ballet while creating custom couture garments that were featured in leading fashion magazines during the early 1940s. Karinska's most important creations were yet to come, but her work in the 1930s was crucial to her development because she was influenced both aesthetically and technically by the great Parisian couturiers such as Vionnet, who, as mentioned above, was renowned for her draping and for cutting fabric on the bias. Vionnet used pliant materials such as silk satins and crepes because they could be sensuously draped around the body. For ballet costumes, Karinska often had to work with heavier materials like

Pink tulle and silver lamé evening dress "for [Vera] Zorina to dance in" by Madeleine Vionnet. *Vogue*, September 15, 1938.

OPPOSITE AND ABOVE: Flesh-pink silk organza, net, and black lace evening dress by Barbara Karinska, New York, ca. 1940.

velvet; nevertheless, she was able to employ "the bias cut for a tightly fitted bodice, where the give and take of the cut could be used to accommodate the aerobic requirements of a dancer's . . . ribcage."[10]

The romantic, sylph-style tutus of *Cotillon* were a harbinger of sweeping changes in fashion to come before and after World War II. Like Vionnet, Coco Chanel, who had rewritten the fashion code in the 1910s by eschewing frothy feminine fashions and wearing her chicly stylized version of menswear instead, was impacted by neo-romantic ballet costumes. Bérard was a close friend of Chanel's and may have been a key source of inspiration for her romantic-style evening clothes. The couturière was also Diaghilev's friend and a patron who supported him financially and even designed costumes for his Ballets Russes.

Throughout the 1930s, Chanel's day clothes retained her signature simplicity and modernity, while her evening dresses became increasingly ornate and extravagant. She chose the materials used to make tutu bodices (satin and velvet) and skirts (fine muslins, lace, and tulle) to craft her bare-shouldered, small-waisted, full-skirted gowns. Among her best romantic, ballet-inspired gowns was "Chagrin d'Amour," made from "tulle as dark as despair" and photographed by Man Ray, who was particularly adept at capturing the neo-romantic spirit. One example that illustrates Bérard's influence on Chanel is a dark blue gown dating to 1937 that was photographed on socialite and fellow Diaghilev supporter Misia Sert.[11] The couturière draped dark blue tulle over an opaque silk base and over Sert's head, like a hood. The tulle is embroidered with metallic sequins in the shape of stars, reminiscent of those Bérard had appliquéd on his *Cotillon* tutus.

Another element of Bérard's *Cotillon* costumes that continued to influence both fashion and ballet through the 1930s and beyond were the long gloves worn by Toumanova. Karinska incorporated them into Balanchine's three "glove ballets": *La Sonnambula* (1946, revived in 1965), *Liebeslieder Walzer* (1960), and especially *La Valse* (1951). In the mid-century, wearing opera-length gloves became a requisite component of a fashionable woman's formal evening ensemble: an evening dress with a fitted bodice and full, long skirt.

ABOVE: "Étoiles" navy-blue tulle evening dress, American licensed copy of a Chanel design, 1937. Collection of Beverley Birks.
OPPOSITE: Art patron Misia Sert in a silk tulle evening dress embroidered with sequins by Coco Chanel, 1937.

ABOVE: Tulle and lace evening dresses by Coco Chanel. *Harper's Bazaar*, September, 1, 1937.
OPPOSITE: Cream and black silk and lace evening dresses by Coco Chanel, 1930s.

After the war, this style was associated with Parisian couturiers such as Christian Dior. Decades later, when former New York City Ballet principal Edward Villella became director of the Miami City Ballet, he asked his dancers, "[The] three ladies who open 'La Valse': who are they? You need to know about Dior's 1947 'new look' [sic]." This shorthand comment summed up the enduring influence of Bérard and Dior, Balanchine and Karinska.[12]

Bérard mentored the young Dior. It could be argued that Bérard was at least one of Dior's spiritual fathers when the couturier debuted his 1947 New Look, a major fashion style that, in turn, (re)informed Balanchine's postwar romantic ballets. Bérard was a seminal figure in the cross-pollination between ballet and fashion during the 1930s and 1940s. He created costume designs for the ballet with the same fluidity as he produced fashion illustrations. Along with photographs of his work, editorial spreads of his ballet costume illustrations, such as those for *Symphonie Fantastique*, a work choreographed by Léonide Massine in 1936, appeared in the fashion magazines.[13] Bérard's interdisciplinary output demonstrated the close relationship between the arts and fashion that continued into the 1950s.

Even before the onset of World War II, male couturiers such as Edward Molyneux, Mainbocher, and Robert Piguet created a range of ballet-style gowns. The Swiss-born Piguet began his career at Bally before opening his own house in Paris in 1933. Best remembered for training Christian Dior and Hubert de Givenchy and for his legendary perfumes such as Fracas and Bandit, Piguet was among the elite mid-century Parisian couturiers who fully embraced the romantic revival. The December 1938 issue of British *Vogue* features his "Le Lac des Cygnes" (Swan Lake) evening gown. The bodice, made of black velvet, sits atop a full, white tulle skirt and is dramatically covered with two white-feathered wings positioned over the bust and extending over the shoulders.

The British were equally smitten with neo-romanticism. Its impact on ballet and fashion was clearly evident in the 1936 production of *Apparitions*. Choreographed by Frederick Ashton to music by Franz Liszt, with the female lead performed by seventeen-year-old Margot Fonteyn, the ballet

was a story of unattainable love. The charming costumes were designed by Cecil Beaton and executed by Barbara Karinska, who moved between Paris and London in the 1930s. Fonteyn's ball-scene costume was long and full, and consisted of layers of tulle, with "masks and skulls . . . buried among its flowery excesses."[14]

Like *Cotillon* in France, *Apparitions* illustrated a link between ballet and fashion in England. Fonteyn's long, full tulle skirt was mirrored in those designed by Britain's leading couturier, Norman Hartnell. Among the most famous examples of his sequined and tiered tulle gowns were the one photographed on actress Gertrude Lawrence by Man Ray for the December 1936 issue of *Harper's Bazaar* and the one worn by the Queen Mother, photographed by Cecil Beaton in 1939. Their filmy translucence and billowing silhouettes, frosted with finely embroidered metallic sequins, found their way into popular cultural media well beyond the rarefied world of ballet. For example, memorable costumes by Hollywood's leading designer, Adrian, include his incandescent gowns in films such as *Camille* (1936) and *San Francisco* (1936), as well as the costume for Glinda, the Good Witch of the North, in *The Wizard of Oz* (1939). Perhaps there was a reciprocal influence of Hollywood on ballet design; Glinda's gown and crown look strikingly similar to a Cecil Beaton costume worn by Tanaquil Le Clercq in Frederick Ashton's 1950 ballet, *Illuminations*.

Balletic influence on British fashion before and after World War II can also be seen in the work of Charles James. In 1934 an image of a James gown appeared in British *Harper's Bazaar*. The sitter, Mrs. Ronald Armstrong-Jones (later known as Anne, Countess of Rosse), was "swathed in spirals of pink and black tulle."[15] The use of tulle to accentuate the balletic quality of James's designs continued into the 1950s. Examples include his "Swan" ball gown of 1949, initially designed for actress Jennifer Jones, which is made of black chiffon and tulle draped across the bodice and upper skirt. Even more dramatic was his 1954 "Butterfly" gown, made with white silk satin and chiffon. Created for Mrs. William Randolph Hearst, it was overlaid with twenty-five yards of yellow, orange, and topaz tulle. A rare James foray

into ready-to-wear also resulted in a ballet-inspired gown. The skirt of his 1952 "Infanta," or "Williamsburg," dress consisted of numerous layers of multicolored tulle: black over rust, yellow, green, beige, and brown. The effect is similar to the multicolored layers of tulle employed by Karinska for the costumes in *La Valse*.

OPPOSITE: Sadler's Wells teenage dancer Margot Fonteyn in Frederick Ashton's *Apparitions*, 1936. Costume design by Cecil Beaton.
ABOVE: Queen Elizabeth (the Queen Mother) in an embroidered silk tulle gown by Norman Hartnell, 1939.

OPPOSITE AND ABOVE: *La Valse* costume, re-created by Marc Happel based on the 1951 original by Barbara Karinska for New York City Ballet.

New York City Ballet
dancers in a 2009
production of *La Valse*.
Costumes re-created
by Marc Happel based
on the 1951 originals
by Barbara Karinska.

OPPOSITE: Silk chiffon and satin "Swan" evening dress, designed by Charles James for entertainer Lisa Kirk, 1954–55.
ABOVE: Anne, Countess of Rosse, in a silk tulle evening dress and wrap by Charles James. British *Harper's Bazaar*, November 1934.

In 1937 Charles James created another ballet-inspired gown, "La Sylphide." Worn by clients such as Anne, Countess of Rosse, and American debutante Esme O'Brien, the evening dress was made from yards of silk organza held in place by a small, seductively curved satin corselet that laced up the back. The skirt's simplicity was balanced by a deeply dramatic swag of organza that draped across the chest and enveloped an abundant bouquet of silk roses. The dress's exuberant romanticism is evident and, as its name suggests, may well have been inspired by the revived interest in the first "Sylphide," Marie Taglioni.

The strong influence of ballet on fashion and vice versa in the mid-century has continued into the twentieth-first century, particularly by those who understand the traditional beauty of both art forms. One compelling and poignant example are the costumes created by Marc Happel, director of costumes at New York City Ballet, for the revival of Balanchine's 1950 ballet *Symphony in C*, originally called *Le Palais Cristal* (The Crystal Palace). The work is one of NYCB's signature ballets, and in 2010 the company's director, Peter Martins, wanted a redesign of Karinska's original famous white and black costumes. According to Happel, who more often than not is charged with implementing the visions of others, Martins's only condition was his desire for a more modern, yet timeless, look.

Happel took inspiration for the ornamentation that covers his tutus from Christian Dior's 1949 "Junon" evening gown. It was named for the Roman goddess (Juno in English), whose symbol was the peacock. Dior captured the feathery essence of the bird in the tiered and scalloped layers of the skirt, which are embroidered with iridescent sequins in colors that transition from pale, shimmery tones to dark teal blue, creating an ombré effect. Interestingly, another Dior work with a similar but more saturated color palette and more three-dimensional embroidery techniques was made for Margot Fonteyn. Designed in 1950, the "Debussy" gown consists of three pieces: a fitted, strapless bodice; a slim, tulip-shaped skirt; and a matching overskirt made of tulle.

A gown by Cristóbal Balenciaga inspired the cut of the Happel-designed bodice. Made of pale pink satin, with silver

ABOVE: Ivory silk organza and satin "La Sylphide" debutante dress with pink silk roses by Charles James, London, 1937.
OPPOSITE: Bodice of Sadler's Wells prima ballerina Margot Fonteyn's "Debussy" embroidered evening ensemble by Christian Dior, spring/summer 1950.

thread embroidery, the Balenciaga top is paired with a full, pink silk tulle skirt. The gown was prominently featured in *Harper's Bazaar*, modeled by Dovima and photographed by Richard Avedon (see pages 4–5). Not only does the couture dress look like a ballerina's costume, but it also resembles one designed by Oliver Messel and worn by Margot Fonteyn for the Sadler's Wells 1946 production of *The Sleeping Beauty*.

Ornamented with Swarovski crystals, the colors of Happel's *Symphony in C* costumes are considerably subtler than those of "Junon" and "Debussy," as he toned down the iridescent purples and incorporated a light touch of blue to echo the stage scrim. The hundreds of thousands of crystals used in the making of the more than forty skirts sit atop a modified version of the powder-puff tutu created for the original *Symphony in C*. Happel notes that the new tutus are made from fourteen layers of tulle and are scalloped à la Dior, giving the costumes an even lighter look. And they are just as ravishing as the couture original.

Throughout the late 1940s and 1950s, Parisian couture echoed the look of postwar classical ballet costumes. Christian Dior, along with Pierre Balmain and Jacques Fath, designed a continuous stream of evening gowns with strapless bodices atop full skirts made from layers of tulle and other filmy fabrics. Even the fashion shows chez Dior were balletic. Reportedly, house models were taught how to stand and walk in a classical ballet manner. As the models brushed by the seated attendees, they twirled.

The Paris Opera Ballet, the world's oldest professional dance company and school, also produced an impressive list of dancers, including Jean Babilée, Zizi Jeanmaire, and Yvette Chauviré. The latter was not only one of the greatest French ballerinas of her era, but she also gained some international renown when the 1938 film *La Mort du Cygne* (The Death of the Swan), or *The Ballerina* for English-speaking audiences, was distributed worldwide. But the Paris Opera Ballet, with its rigid training and staid programming, had little influence outside of France. A small number of more experimental talents such as Serge Lifar and especially Roland Petit, who founded the Ballets des Champs-Élysées, generated interest and publicity. Even though French ballet influenced the

powerful couture industry, its impact on fashion could not compete with its British and American counterparts, especially after World War II.

The neo-romantic style that dominated fashion and dance from the mid-1930s through the 1950s was personified by one of the greatest ballerinas of her era, Margot Fonteyn (1919–1991). An heir to Anna Pavlova's legacy, Fonteyn was also the embodiment of British ballet. She was both a talented technician and a great actress; moreover, her body and carriage exemplified the look of the modern ballerina: she was elegant with perfect proportions and danced in an unadorned, restrained style. Seemingly delicate, Fonteyn possessed great strength, as evidenced by her ramrod-straight back and near-flawless technical control. Already a rising star in Great Britain during the 1930s and a national idol during the war, she became an international phenomenon after her 1949 debut in New York as Aurora in *The Sleeping Beauty*.

Fonteyn carried on the Russian classical tradition of ballet, but she was also an ideal model of contemporary fashion. Postwar styles evocative of the nineteenth century were perfect on the slender dancers who, in turn, modernized these historically inspired fashions. When Sadler's Wells (the precursor to the Royal Ballet) embarked on its 1949 tour of the United States and Canada, the company highlighted not only British dance but also high fashion, and the Incorporated Society of London Fashion Designers (ISLFD) used the tour as a selling tool. Members of the ISLFD such as Norman Hartnell, Digby Morton, and Bianca Mosca produced clothes and accessories for the company's female dancers. They also created special garments for Fonteyn and other ballerinas, including Pamela May, Beryl Grey, and Moira Shearer, who, in addition to their grueling performance schedule on the sold-out tour, participated in fashion shoots for American magazines and newspapers. Fonteyn, for example, was photographed by Cecil Beaton for *Vogue* in a Bianca Mosca black evening gown (see page 134).

The collaboration between British designers and dancers was not sustained, however, at least not by Fonteyn. She had a great fondness for the City of Lights, especially after the war, when Great Britain was still reeling from the damage

Pale pink tulle and embroidered satin gown designed by Cristóbal Balenciaga, licensed by Hattie Carnegie, 1950. Collection of Beverley Birks.

ABOVE: Royal Ballet prima ballerina Margot Fonteyn's Princess Aurora costume from *The Sleeping Beauty*, 1960s. Originally designed in 1946 by Oliver Messel.
OPPOSITE: Costume for George Balanchine's *Symphony in C*, designed by Mark Happel in 2012 for New York City Ballet.

outfits. . . . I bought some ravishing dresses from Dior and of course, ordered my wedding dress there."[16] For her wedding in 1954, the ballerina wore a dress of silver-gray silk faille with a voluminous, mid-calf-length skirt and three-quarter-length sleeves. It was topped with a pewter-gray silk faille coat, lined in silver-gray faille to match the dress (see pages 152–53). The ensemble, which included custom-made accessories, sold at auction in 2000 for more than $20,000.

Dozens of other fashion objects worn by Fonteyn are now in the Fashion Museum in Bath, England. Most of her wardrobe was designed by French couturiers (initially Dior, but after his death in 1957, Yves Saint Laurent) and consisted most likely of samples purchased at the end of the season.[17] Some items, such as a beautifully simple Dior gown that Fonteyn wore on her Australia tour in 1957 (now in the collection of the Victoria & Albert Museum), have bodices that echo her postwar Black Swan costume. And Fonteyn may have been one of the inspirations for Dior's "Cygne Noir" (Black Swan) evening gown, designed for his autumn/winter 1949–50 collection.

Like Kschessinska and Pavlova before her, Margot Fonteyn must have understood the power of fashion, especially for a dancer. In 1965 she was listed as one of the ten best-dressed women in the world. Her elegant dancing and her wardrobe were enhanced by her titles. She was appointed prima ballerina assoluta by the Queen and was awarded a Dame Grand Cross of the Most Excellent Order of the British Empire. But Fonteyn was also a sensuous and complicated artist whose offstage persona was both sexier and more progressive than most knew.

One of the most evocative portrayals of the ballerina was by the Argentine-born Surrealist artist Leonor Fini. In addition to painting, Fini designed sets and costumes for both masked balls and the theater. In fact, it was when Fini was working on the sets and costumes of Roland Petit's 1948 ballet, *Les Demoiselles de la Nuit*, that Fonteyn and Fini met. They eventually became friends, but not before they waged war over a custom-made mask that the ballerina refused to wear. Fonteyn recalled in her autobiography that the "perfect cat-like mask complete of pink nose, mustache and all" left her unable to emote with her "head locked in a box-cat. A love duet

wrought by Nazi bombs and from severe shortages of basic goods. Fonteyn traveled to Paris and the South of France frequently to dance, train, and vacation in the postwar years. And she opted to buy her clothes at the house of Dior in Paris. Introduced to the couturier by the French dancer and choreographer Roland Petit shortly after Dior's debut collection in 1947, Fonteyn recalled that the "Maison Dior decided to take me under its wing, and I bought one of the first season's

ABOVE: Sadler's Wells prima ballerina Margot Fonteyn as Princess Aurora in *The Sleeping Beauty*, ca. 1949.
OPPOSITE: "Cygne Noir" silk satin and velvet evening dress by Christian Dior, autumn/winter 1949–50.

was out of the question. I felt grotesque." After threatening to burn down the theater, Fini relented and reworked the mask.

Later in 1948, Fonteyn and Fini vacationed together in the South of France, along with Roland Petit and Fonteyn's best American friend, Joy Brown (née Williams), a fellow dancer and a member of Petit's company at the time.[18] Though both dancers were lovely and had enviable physiques, they had markedly different coloring and, according to Fini's portrayal of them, temperaments. Standing in profile and wearing an abbreviated corset that exposes her buttocks, with a voluminous mane of hair framing her upper body, Fonteyn is an untamed seductress. Brown, seated with a long-haired mantle draped across her torso and an array of what appear to be tree roots and animal horns balanced on her head, looks like an ethereal princess from a pagan tribe. This provocative dual portrait of mid-century ballerinas is antithetical to the refined image so many tried to burnish. With no tutus or tiaras, they are neither proper nor classical in their surreal costumes. This painting is an intimate glimpse that reveals another dimension of the ballerina beyond her refined, couture-clad persona.[19]

Fonteyn was not the only British ballerina to wear Parisian couture and push the boundaries of her creativity. In the late 1940s Moira Shearer, a fellow principal at the Sadler's Wells Ballet, became the most famous ballet dancer in the world because of her starring role in the British film *The Red Shoes*. Produced by Michael Powell and Emeric Pressburger in 1948, it is a modern adaptation of Hans Christian Andersen's classic fairy tale. Featuring outstanding dance sequences, it is considered by many to be one of the best films of its time and possibly the best ballet movie ever made.

A key element of *The Red Shoes* is its gorgeous costumes. The film credits "Miss Shearer's Dresses" to couturiers "Jacques Fath of Paris" and "Mattli of London," and fellow dancer "Mlle. Tcherina's Dresses" to "Carven of Paris." The wardrobe credit goes to Dorothy Edwards, who, one assumes, designed and oversaw the dance costumes and rehearsal clothes. *The Red Shoes* is a visual dream and a hymn to excess, clearly welcome to audiences who had endured the devastating effects of the Depression and World War II. Though all the costumes, both "real" clothes and stage cos-

tumes, are beautiful, one evening gown by Fath, with its iridescent blue-green color and silky sheen, is a standout that enhances Shearer's rich, bright auburn hair and pale complexion. Topped with a matching cape, the silhouette of the layered and tiered tulle gown is reminiscent of those designed by Hartnell for the Queen Mother before the war (see page 89), while the dynamic layering of fabric evokes Karinska's costumes and Charles James's gowns. Shearer's crowning touch is just that—a small, jeweled crown à la Kschessinska.

British ballerinas were not the only ones to wear haute couture. A unique American example was dancer, choreographer, and company director Ruth Page. Like Fonteyn, Page opted to wear Christian Dior in the 1950s, and her impressive collection also found its way into a public arts institution, specifically the Chicago History Museum (CHM). Born in Indianapolis in 1899, Page began her ballet career dancing with Anna Pavlova's traveling company in 1918, when it was on tour in South America. In 1925 she was hired by Sergei Diaghilev and was the first and only American to dance with the original Ballets Russes. Like her British colleague Ninette de Valois, Page eventually returned to her roots—in her case the Midwest—to establish a school and company. She founded

OPPOSITE: *Elles aiment se déguiser* (They Love to Dress Up), portrait of Joy Williams and Margot Fonteyn by Leonor Fini, oil on canvas, 1948.
ABOVE: Film still of Sadler's Wells ballerina Moira Shearer wearing an evening ensemble by Jacques Fath, *The Red Shoes*, 1948.

the Chicago Opera Ballet and later established the Ruth Page Foundation, an organization dedicated to fostering young talent in the performing arts.

Throughout her long life, Page lived by her own words: "Be adventurous, be chic." The CHM's collection of her clothes includes seventeen dresses designed by Christian Dior dating from the late 1940s to the couturier's death in 1957. Page's marriage to attorney Thomas Hart Fisher gave her the wherewithal to indulge her penchant for couture. "At the time she was purchasing them, 17 Dior dresses were an enormous investment," said CHM curator Tim Long, "because each cost as much as a new car."

Like Page, Maria Tallchief made Chicago her home after her illustrious dancing career came to an end, and she, too, was a Dior client, thanks to the largess of her first husband, George Balanchine. In her autobiography, Tallchief notes that "George bought me the two Dior dresses" while they were working in the City of Lights. Shortly after the war, he was invited by the Paris Opera Ballet as a guest choreographer. And she was the first American to dance with that company, which she did to great acclaim.

According to the CHM's donor records, Tallchief and Balanchine attended Dior's momentous premier on February 12, 1947. At the presentation of his collection, the couturier himself escorted the ballerina and the choreographer to their seats. Balanchine's first Dior purchase (there would be more in the coming years) was named "Maxim," after Dior's favorite restaurant. Tallchief wore the dress when she received the 1953 Woman of the Year award from President Dwight D. Eisenhower.[20] Made of black wool crepe, it is a chic dress with three-quarter-length sleeves, fitted waistline, and an A-line skirt; it is dramatically ornamented with a large velvet bow placed at the center of the neckline and two large patch pockets that sit atop each hip. Tallchief explained that the wife of violinist Nathan Milstein, Therese, asked to borrow "the basic black [one] so that her dressmaker there could copy it."[21] This description implies that two dresses of different colors were bought at the same time. However, the only known Tallchief Dior garments, now in the CHM, are both black. If Balanchine purchased another dress from Dior's debut 1947

ABOVE: NYCB ballerina Maria Tallchief's black wool crepe and silk velvet dress, "Maxim," by Christian Dior, 1947.
OPPOSITE: Black synthetic tulle and silk faille evening dress by Christian Dior, autumn 1955.

OPPOSITE: American ballerina Ruth Page's silk tulle evening dress embroidered with sequins and rhinestones by Christian Dior, 1953.
ABOVE: British ballerina Alicia Markova's silk faille "Tambourin" evening dress by Christian Dior, autumn/winter 1955.

collection for Tallchief, as she herself recalled, no information about it has come to light.

The other Dior dress donated to the CHM by Tallchief is, according to the records, a two-piece black silk faille cocktail dress designed in 1954. If the records are correct, it was created two years after the annulment of her marriage to Balanchine and possibly around the time of her second marriage (to a pilot, which ended in divorce). Her third and final marriage, in 1956, was to Henry D. Paschen Jr., an executive at a Chicago construction company. Did she buy the dress herself? Or was it purchased by one of her other husbands?

In addition to the rather obscure details about its acquisition, the CHM records note that "the donor does not remember altering this garment," although "there are signs of alterations throughout the bodice, waist and skirt hem. The original lining to the bodice has been replaced with a sheer fabric allowing visibility of the interior craftsmanship and alterations." The records also note that a "piece of twine and a metal 'seal' hang from the interior side seam, which signifies that import tax was paid on this garment." This information indicates that the dress was made and purchased in Paris, then legally shipped to the United States. Tallchief may have been a star, but her income would still have been modest. It seems unlikely that she paid for the dress herself.

Balanchine also selected Tallchief's hallmark perfume. Like the couture clothes, it, too, would outlast the marriage.

Scene from *Treize Danses*, choreographed by Roland Petit with costumes by Christian Dior, 1947.

Tallchief noted: "One afternoon, we went to the House of Guerlain. George wanted to choose a perfume for me. We sampled several before he settled on L'Heure Bleue (the expression the French have for twilight), a beautiful, subtle fragrance that I still use today. George dabbed some on my neck below my ear and lowered his head. His lips softly touched mine. The solemnity with which he conducted the perfume ritual, and the unexpected display of affection, was a surprise and was more fulfilling because of that. I felt gratified and loved."[22]

Aside from creating haute couture that celebrity ballerinas adored, Dior designed what the critic and historian Richard Buckle described as "very elaborate dresses" for Roland Petit's 1947 ballet *Treize Danses*. Against a simple set of "plain gray flats and orange lanterns," Buckle wrote, the "fantastic, ingenious and beautiful" garments were "too

exquisitely conceived to be effective in a theater." Despite this reservation, he described them in detail: "They were perfect fancy-dresses, mostly in black and white, with some purple here and there, and brown-pink. One was conscious of the shine of satin, the flash of sequins and diamante, the originality of material printed like leopard-skin, the extravagance of aigrettes."[23] Buckle's assessment that high fashion is too finely detailed for the stage is held by many performing-arts experts. Yet Dior's talent was readily acknowledged.

Pierre Balmain has also been credited with designing costumes for several ballets, although records of his work are less well documented than Dior's, and what records there are can be confusing. Several sources state that French ballerina Janine Charrat, a star of the Ballets des Champs-Élysées and a choreographer, collaborated with Balmain on

Christian Dior's costumes for *Treize Danses*, 1947, illustrated by Christian Bérard.

the costumes for one of her earliest works, *La Femme et Son Ombre* (The Woman and Her Shadow). It debuted on June 15, 1948. Of the three major publications on the couturier, including two monographic studies and his autobiography, only one of them mentions this work and none includes images of the production.

Balmain supposedly designed the costumes for one of the more famous French ballets produced during this time, *Grand Pas Classique*. With choreography by Victor Gsovsky, it debuted at the Théâtre des Champs-Élysées in November 1949. The costume created for the great French ballerina Yvette Chauviré appears to have been made of pale satin with a fitted bodice. Dark tulle bands lie across the shoulders and the tutu has a small circumference, edged with dark trimming. Though Balmain is named as the designer on a website dedicated to Russian émigré photographer Serge Lido and dancer Wladimir Skouratoff, no corroborating evidence has come to light.

Balmain is also credited with designing costumes for the international company Grand Ballet du Marquis de Cuevas, specifically for George Balanchine's *Pas de Trois Classique*, essentially a restaging of the pas de trois from the nineteenth-century Russian ballet *Paquita*. Starring Marjorie Tallchief (Maria's younger sister), Rosella Hightower, and André Eglevsky, the work debuted on August 9, 1948, at the Royal Opera House, Covent Garden, in London.[24]

One of Balmain's biographers credits the costumes for yet another ballet, the celebrated revival of *The Sleeping Beauty* danced by Margot Fonteyn beginning in 1946, to Balmain.[25] The author does not mention where this production was staged, but if true, most likely it was in Paris. This is the only logical conclusion because the costumes for the famed Sadler's Wells production of *The Sleeping Beau*ty—the same production that made Fonteyn an international star when she danced the role throughout North America—were designed by Oliver Messel.

Though Balmain's costume design may not be accurately documented, his work as a couturier clearly echoed ballerinas' costumes, perhaps more than that of any major designer of his time. Several examples in the collection of

The Museum at FIT illustrate the range of Balmain's ballet-influenced gowns. One of the most basic is an evening dress with a full skirt made of ivory tulle and a bodice delicately overlaid with the same material. Another is an evening ensemble consisting of a full, graphite-gray tulle skirt topped with a practice-style knitted cardigan of the same color. The sweater is dressed up with black sequins and glass beads embroidered on the edges of the collar, along the center front opening, and in three horizontal bands that descend down each arm. Decidedly more dramatic and balletic is a corseted evening ensemble that features a blue silk bodice and underskirt with a smoky gray velvet overskirt. Elements of eighteenth-century fashion are evident in the trapunto-stitched corset and the full-hipped, panniered skirt. But the bust, draped with deeply pleated arcs of fabric, possesses the theatricality of stage costume with couture detailing.

Another theatrical element that figures prominently in Balmain's ballet-inspired gowns is the use of feathers. References to birds abound in ballet. Numerous variations and full-length works involve feathered creatures, including the Bluebird pas de deux in *The Sleeping Beauty*, the Hunt of the Larks in *Harlequinade*, *The Firebird*, *The Two Pigeons*, Pavlova's *The Dying Swan* solo, and perhaps the most famous ballet in history, *Swan Lake*. Though some of Balmain's gowns, such as the off-white tulle creation beautifully ornamented with sprays of faux-pheasant feathers in the private collection of fashion editor Hamish Bowles, may have no connection to a specific ballet, two reference white-feathered tutus quite explicitly. One, in The Museum at FIT's collection, is decidedly balletic with its pink satin corset and white tulle skirt covered with curled white chicken feathers. An even more literal example of the ballerina as bird is in the collection of the Victoria & Albert Museum. Described as a debutante gown, it more likely belonged to a wealthy American expatriate who married a Brit and made London her home. Made of off-white silk with a gossamer overlay of organza, the gown is flamboyantly embroidered with fine metallic sequins in an ostrich-feather pattern, a motif that echoes the real ostrich plumes that dramatically cover the bodice and upper part of the skirt.

Off-white tulle evening dress by Pierre Balmain, ca. 1955.

LEFT: Blue silk
taffeta and gray
velvet evening dress
by Pierre Balmain,
ca. 1951.
OPPOSITE: Gray
evening ensemble
consisting of an
embroidered wool
sweater and silk
chiffon skirt by Pierre
Balmain, ca. 1952.

ABOVE AND OPPOSITE: Gold-painted white tulle debutante gown with painted velvet "feathers."
Made for the Honorable Lucinda Lambton by Pierre Balmain, 1960. Collection of Hamish Bowles.

Like Dior, Balmain gave ballet-related names to a few of his designs. For his winter 1955–56 collection, for instance, he created the "Taglioni" cocktail dress. Now in the permanent collection of the Palais Galliera, Musée de la Mode, in Paris, its draped bodice and full skirt are crafted of cream silk satin, and the skirt is ornamented with an embroidered floral motif by the renowned embroidery atelier Hurel.

In ballet, as in fashion, color is as important an element as silhouette and materials. The predominant color of the Romantic ballets of the 1830s and 1840s is white. Known as *ballets blancs* (white ballets), they often feature an assemblage of up to several dozen young corps de ballet members dressed in identical white costumes who dance in unison, serving both as the human backdrop to the lead performers and as a precisely timed, unified group that advances and enhances the often-tragic storyline. Perhaps the definitive *ballet blanc* is the second act of the 1841 classic *Giselle*, in which the Wilis—young women who have met an early death because they were betrayed by deceitful lovers—attempt to avenge a recently wronged girl who has joined their ranks.

In Russia, innovative variations of the *ballet blanc* continued to be created until the late nineteenth century. One of the most brilliant and haunting is the second act of *La Bayadère* (or Indian temple dancer). Some two dozen dancers dressed in white tutus with translucent scarves draped between their chignons and fingers are the vision of the lead male dancer's hallucinogenic dream. Masterfully choreographed by Marius Petipa, this act is among the greatest in the classical ballet canon. In the second act of *Swan Lake*, also choreographed by Petipa, the corps, swathed in white, feather-covered tutus and headdresses, is equally compelling and even more famous. Together, the dances of Wilis, bayadères, and swans in white are among ballet's crowning achievements.

The image of the ballerina as swan was cemented after Pavlova debuted *The Dying Swan* solo in 1905. It was her most famous work, thanks to her extraordinary interpretation and the wide distribution of photographs of her in the white-feathered costume (see page 48). For her debut in the role of Odette, the swan queen in *Swan Lake*, Fonteyn wore a tutu made by Anna Pavlova's dresser, Madame Manya,

widely considered to be the greatest tutu maker of the pre–World War II era. According to one source, it served "as the model for all subsequent tutus, and the style of all the Sadler's Wells' tutus thereafter derives directly from Margot's original Pavlova model."[26] Covered in a plethora of feathers and flourishes, it resembled Pavlova's tutus, especially those made for *The Dying Swan*, and was reminiscent of the Imperial Russian style. But the tutu, like fashion, became much sleeker and more rigid after World War II. In a tribute to the great swan ballerina, who died in January 1931, Elsa Schiaparelli designed a striking white, coq-feathered cape for herself and wore it in May of that year to the gala reopening of Les Ambassadeurs restaurant in Paris. Interestingly, in 1917,

OPPOSITE: Silk and organza evening gown with ostrich plumes and embroidered with sequins by Pierre Balmain, embroidery by Lesage, Paris, ca. 1950.
ABOVE: Man Ray portrait of Elsa Schiaparelli in a feathered cape inspired by Anna Pavlova, 1931.

lean, articulated lines of his dancers and still stand as radical departures from the classics that preceded them.

Black has also come to define one of the best-known roles in the entire classical canon: Odile, or as she is now known, the Black Swan, in *Swan Lake*. Originally created in 1877, the full-length work to the score by Tchaikovsky was dramatically overhauled in 1895. Since then, the dual roles of the virtuous Odette, also called the White Swan, and the evil Odile are perhaps the most demanding and understandably celebrated a ballerina can undertake. Yet Odile was not originally dressed in black. The costume was at times multicolored and iridescent. Ballet historian Robert Greskovic contends that the black tutu was first used during the 1941 Ballet Russe de Monte Carlo season in New York, with Tamara Toumanova dancing the lead, but evidence suggests that some ballerinas wore black costumes much earlier.

One of the reasons for this late change may be the fact that black swans do not exist in Europe, Asia, Africa, or the Americas. Australia is the indigenous home of the black swan. Could members of the Ballet Russe de Monte Carlo have seen black swans for the first time while touring Down Under before World War II? And did the Australians and New Zealanders, ardent dance enthusiasts who created the Pavlova, a fruit-topped meringue and cream dessert, have any influence on the new costume? Whatever the actual history of the black Odile costume may be, couturier Christian Dior's "Cygne Noir" gown and Hollywood costumier Howard Greer's "Odile" evening dress, dating to about 1950, were clearly inspired by this now famous ballet costume.

Perhaps the color most closely associated with ballet is pink. There are several hues, from pale flesh to what is called "ballet pink" (cooler but also pale), in which nearly all the tights and silk satin pointe shoes are rendered. From the first knitted garments worn close to the body in the early nineteenth century, the idea was to match the color of the dancers' skin tone. This blending of flesh and undergarment both hid the naked body and highlighted the sculpted human form. The modern pale pink satin pointe shoe, first worn by the nineteenth-century Romantic ballerinas, were initially slightly reinforced high-fashion flat slippers with silk ribbon

when Schiaparelli was in Cuba, she was often mistaken for Pavlova, whom she resembled, and who was performing in Havana at that time.[27]

Black has also played an important role in ballet. Though it is perhaps more often worn by male dancers, particularly those dancing noble character or villain roles, it is also paired with white in many of George Balanchine's modern ballets. His aptly named black-and-white ballets celebrate the

ABOVE: Bluebird costume by Léon Bakst for the Ballets Russes production of *The Sleeping Princess*, 1921.
OPPOSITE: "Odile" black silk tulle evening dress embroidered with sequins by Howard Greer, ca. 1951. Collection of Beverley Birks.

ties. This fusion of body, clothing, and accessory extended the visual line of the increasingly exposed leg.

Though white, black, and pink were prevalent in both ballet and high fashion before World War II, Diaghilev's 1921 *Sleeping Princess* and its abbreviated offshoot, *Aurora's Wedding*, may have been the catalyst in the West for the popularization of two trendy colors on the eve of global conflict: a vibrant shade of blue and pale purple, or lilac. From the 1890 debut of the original *Sleeping Beauty* in Russia, critics consistently lauded the production's gorgeous sets and costumes. With its bright and sometimes clashing pigments, *Beauty* recalibrated ballet's palette and made an indelible impression on Sergei Diaghilev and his coterie of costume and set designers.

One of the signature dances in *Beauty* is the Bluebird pas de deux, based on a fairy tale. Petipa choreographed the male part especially for Enrico Cecchetti, the Italian virtuoso who was instrumental in transforming the traditionally conservative roles of the male dancer into bravura parts. His performance as the Bluebird caused a sensation. Done properly, the dancer appeared to hover in the air while executing the demanding *brisés volés*, a series of scissoring beats and small jumps that shift continuously forward and back. Enhancing the Bluebird was his costume, colored in a rich shade of blue.

The blue of Léon Bakst's Bluebird costume for Diaghilev's *Sleeping Princess* is remarkably similar to Elsa Schiaparelli's second signature color, "Sleeping Blue" (after her "Shocking Pink"). The presentation of her summer 1940 collection on January 26 featured a "linen jacket trimmed with Sleeping blue velvet" and a fitted black evening dress topped with a jet-trimmed bolero in the same blue. The latter ensemble was a hit. A full-page color illustration of the dress and bolero by Surrealist artist Leonor Fini appeared in the March 15, 1940, issue of *Harper's Bazaar*, and a photograph of it by Leslie Gill was published in the April 1940 issue. This original design is now part of fashion editor Hamish Bowles's extraordinary private collection. The color celebrated Schiaparelli's latest perfume, aptly named Sleeping. Described as a heavy, sugary scent with a touch of vanilla, Sleeping was bottled in a

Baccarat crystal candlestick with a lighted taper and a cone-shaped extinguisher. The bottle and taper were depicted in numerous advertisements illustrated by Marcel Vertès between 1940 and 1948, and the perfume was sold in a box depicting either a miniature eighteenth-century drawing room or a royal canopied bed. The similarity between *Beauty*'s sets and Schiaparelli's packaging is unmistakable.

OPPOSITE: "Sleeping Blue" evening jacket by Elsa Schiaparelli, illustrated by Leonor Fini. *Harper's Bazaar*, March 15, 1940.
ABOVE: "Sleeping Blue" bolero jacket by Elsa Schiaparelli, spring 1940. Collection of Hamish Bowles.

Dilys Blum, the curator of costume and textiles at the Philadelphia Museum of Art, cites 1940 as the year of the perfume launch, whereas Schiaparelli biographer Palmer White claims it was 1938. Lending credence to White's dating is the fact that Schiaparelli incorporated vibrant blue into her winter 1938–39 collection; the January 1939 issue of *Harper's Bazaar* features her "turquoise velvet dress . . . embellished with sapphires and silver-thread embroidery." In a later issue of *Harper's Bazaar* that year, Marcel Vertès illustrated a male dancer, costumed as Cinderella's prince, in a rich blue tunic embellished with fleurs-de-lis. Vertès also illustrated two advertisements for Shocking perfume. In one, a dancer-like figure in a blue jacket draws back a stage curtain; in the other, a young woman wears a cloak covered in candles. The candle is symbolic in another popular Russian ballet, *The Nutcracker*. (Elements of *The Nutcracker* were incorporated into the Western productions of *The Sleeping Beauty*.) Was Schiaparelli inspired by the fairy tale pas de deux within the larger fairy tale ballet? *Aurora's Wedding* was performed hundreds of time by the Ballets Russes and its successor companies in the 1920s and 1930s, providing ample opportunity for Schiaparelli to have seen it.

Another color closely associated with *The Sleeping Beauty* is lilac, the signature hue of the story's savior, the Lilac Fairy. By choosing this color, *Beauty*'s librettist, choreographer, composer, and designer evoked the flower's ancient and modern symbolism. Since antiquity, lilacs have been harbingers of spring, or rebirth. For the Victorians, in their "language of flowers," or floriography, purple lilacs symbolize the feelings of first love, while white lilacs represent youthful innocence. All these meanings are apt, as the Lilac Fairy mitigates the deadly spell cast by the evil fairy Carabosse. Angered that she was not invited to Princess Aurora's christening, Carabosse shows up at the event and places a curse on the infant: on her sixteenth birthday, Aurora will prick her finger on a spindle and die. The Lilac Fairy cannot undo the spell, but she alters it; instead of death, the spindle will cause Aurora to fall into a deep sleep for a century, to be awakened by the kiss of a handsome prince.

In the original 1890 production, the lilac's symbolism was extended to the costume design. Though most of the non-dancing female characters wear eighteenth-century-style panniers, the Lilac Fairy wears a costume in the "corseted, bustled, *tapissier* (upholsterer) style of the contemporary couturier Charles Worth"[28] in the second act. This modish purple costume was more than a fashion statement. Audiences understood that purple was traditionally associated with royalty because it was a rare and precious commodity (the extraction of purple dye from the glands of mollusks was a highly labor-intensive, expensive process). But the royal connotation of purple waned during the Victorian era, after the discovery in 1856 of a lilac-colored synthetic dye called mauveine that was easily produced. In 1862, the year after Prince Albert died, Queen Victoria was seen wearing this pale purple color to the Royal Exhibition, and lilac soon became the color of half mourning. Black clothing and veils associated with the first stage of mourning were gradually replaced by garments in shades of purple, as well as shades of gray.

Strict mourning rituals fell out of favor by the end of nineteenth century, and fashion embraced the new-found youthful spirit of lilac. By the 1930s, any connection of lilac to mourning attire had gone, and designers were creating warm-weather gowns embroidered with lilacs or ornamented with large lilac corsages. New York fashion retailers placed advertisements of their exclusive designs in the spring 1940 issues of *Harper's Bazaar*. Bergdorf Goodman celebrated its "Full Moon Skirt of silk leaves and lilacs on stiff coarse net," and Stein & Blaine promoted a gown with the caption: "It's Lilac Time—fragrant exquisiteness." Editorial features in *Harper's Bazaar* that summer featured gowns by Alix (Madame Grès) and Chanel that were accessorized with lilac bouquets and corsages. Fashion's infatuation with lilacs coincided with the 1939 Sadler's Wells debut production of *The Sleeping Beauty* in London and numerous versions of *Aurora's Wedding* that were presented by the Ballet Russe de Monte Carlo and the New York–based Ballet Theatre throughout the 1930s and early 1940s. Lilac and other, similar pastel hues remained popular well after the war, as seen in beautiful gowns by couturiers such as Antonio de Castillo for Lanvin.

Just as couturiers freely adapted elements from ballet costumes, including silhouette, color, and materials,

Lilac tulle cocktail dress by Antonio Castillo for Lanvin, 1956.

Louis Arpels, a passionate balletomane, commissioned Maurice Duvalet, a French-born designer who had moved to America at the end of World War I, and Jean "John" Rubel, the house's master artisan, who emigrated from Paris prior to World War II, to collaborate on the brooches. Van Cleef & Arpels began producing them soon after it opened its New York City flagship store in 1939.

One of their first creations was the 1941 "Danseuse Espagnole," or Spanish Dancer, brooch, which was made of diamonds, rubies, and emeralds. Legend has it that Rubel was inspired to create this brooch after seeing a group of flamenco dancers at a café on the Lower East Side of Manhattan. But it is also possible that the piece may have been inspired by the "ethnic" divertissements included in a number of full-length ballets, as the dancer's pose on the brooch is absolutely balletic.

Duvalet's meticulously rendered sketches for the brooches included glittering faces, each made from a single, rose-cut diamond, and varied stones for the costumes. He was inspired by marquee ballerinas, both historic and contemporary. In 1942 Van Cleef & Arpels debuted the "Camargo" brooch. Made with diamonds, rubies, and emeralds set in platinum, it was modeled after the ca. 1730 portrait of Marie Camargo by Nicolas Lancret. Around the same, time Duvalet designed the Anna Pavlova brooch. The firm placed an advertisement featuring the Pavlova brooch in the April 1944 issue of *Harper's Bazaar*.[29]

In America, the ballerina brooches were made with precious stones, including diamonds, rubies, emeralds, and sapphires, mounted in platinum. The cachet of the American pieces was enhanced because they reportedly contained gems from the Spanish Crown jewels, taken to Mexico during political unrest and later sold at auction in New York. The French versions of the ballerina brooches differed significantly because the stones were set mainly in gold, and the rubies and sapphires were paired with semiprecious stones such as turquoise instead of diamonds. The brooches remained popular until production in both France and America ceased at the end of the 1960s. During their heyday, a who's who of American jewelry collectors acquired Van Cleef & Arpels ballerina brooches, including Marjorie Merriweather Post, Jessie

so did leading jewelers. Two of the most prevalent dance-inspired types of jewelry were the ballerina cocktail ring and brooch. Born in the 1920s, the aptly named cocktail ring glittered on the fingers of many young, alcohol-swilling patrons of speakeasies, the clandestine bars that sprang up in defiance of Prohibition, the restrictive laws of the Eighteenth Amendment that banned the production and consumption of alcohol in America. The variation known as the ballerina cocktail ring became popular during the mid-twentieth century, when Prohibition was a thing of the past. Large and bold, with a halo of tapered, baguette-cut diamonds shimmering around a large, round center stone, the ballerina cocktail ring, when viewed from above, had the appearance of a flared tutu.

Around the onset of World War II, fine jewelry became more whimsical and experimental. The ballerina brooch was one of the era's memorable inventions. It was created by Van Cleef & Arpels, the illustrious family-run jewelry firm founded in 1896 in Paris. One of the founders' descendants,

[Vera] "Zorina" ballerina brooch made of diamonds and sapphires set in platinum by Van Cleef & Arpels, 1944.

130

Woolworth Donahue, and Barbara Hutton, thus attesting to the elevated status of ballerinas.

Van Cleef & Arpels may also have played a role in the creation of one of the greatest ballets choreographed by George Balanchine, *Jewels*. Around the time of the ballet's premiere in 1967, newspaper articles reported that Claude Arpels had suggested the idea of a ballet based on jewels to Balanchine. Other sources claim that it was the choreographer's own idea and that it came to him on one of his daily walks along Fifth Avenue past the windows of the Van Cleef & Arpels boutique. A friend of the Arpels family, Balanchine was familiar with the jewelry; he supposedly bought a ballerina brooch around 1944 depicting his wife at the time, Vera Zorina, in an arabesque.

Jewels is Balanchine's ode to ballet itself. Ostensibly plotless, it is a three-act, full-length masterpiece of potent choreography, perfect musical selections, and ravishing costumes by Barbara Karinska (see page 31). Laura Jacobs, among other critics, refutes the description of *Jewels* as a "full-length ballet without a plot," noting that "the phrase contains not a glimmer of the ballet's vast holdings. In echoes, allusions, and refractions, it is arguably the richest ballet ever made."[30]

The first part, "Emeralds," is an homage to Romantic French ballet and possesses the feel of a medieval, courtly fairy tale. With music by Gabriel Fauré, two ballerinas (originally Violette Verdy and Mimi Paul) dance in a lush and fragrant landscape, their movement tinged with fleeting poignancy. The second part, "Rubies," is the diametric opposite. Inspired by Balanchine's new homeland, America, it is vibrant and jazzy, and a trio of dancers (originally Patricia McBride, Edward Villella, and Patricia Neary) moves to Igor Stravinsky's syncopated rhythms and discordant sounds with verve, energy, and fractured steps that challenge ballet's classical history. The final part, "Diamonds," is a celebration of the choreographer's Imperial Russian roots. Set to a sweeping Tchaikovsky score, it achieves an exquisite balance between traditional classicism and Balanchine's modernism, revolving around the central female dancer (originally Suzanne Farrell, with whom Balanchine was madly infatuated). Costumes for each part were distinctive: calf-length romantic tutus for "Emeralds"; short, ruffled skirts (which later became flaps)

NYCB "Rubies" costume for George Balanchine's *Jewels*, re-created in 2011 based on the 1967 original by Barbara Karinska.

for "Rubies"; and New York City Ballet's signature powder-puff tutu for "Diamonds." And all were adorned with large, vibrant jewels in green, red, and white, respectively.

Jewels continues to dazzle audiences; it is a mainstay of New York City Ballet and has entered the repertory of companies around the world, including the Paris Opera Ballet and the Mariinsky in St. Petersburg. It is also credited with the revived production of ballerina-inspired jewelry by Van Cleef & Arpels. In 2013 Benjamin Millepied, a former New York City Ballet dancer and director of the Paris Opera Ballet,

and his wife, actress Natalie Portman, who starred in the 2010 movie *Black Swan*, collaborated on the firm's most recent ballerina brooch offering.

Ballet's impact on the fashion world could have reached no loftier height than emulation in jewelry, especially fine jewelry. The most expensive and exclusive of all accessories, jewels set with precious stones have been symbols of regal power, wealth, and prestige since ancient times. Jewelry's mid-century embrace of ballet was a testament to how legitimate and respected ballet had become in the West.

ABOVE: NYCB "Emeralds" costume for George Balanchine's *Jewels*, re-created in 2016 based on the 1967 original by Barbara Karinska.
OPPOSITE: NYCB "Diamonds" costume for George Balanchine's *Jewels*, re-created in 2011 based on the 1967 original by Barbara Karinska.

ENTER THE BALLERINA: MARGOT FONTEYN AND FASHION, 1930s–1960s

ROSEMARY HARDEN

PRIMA BALLERINA ASSOLUTA

"The prima ballerina assoluta of the Royal
Ballet is Dame Margot Fonteyn."[1]

For more than forty years, Dame Margot Fonteyn de Arias (1919–1991) was arguably the most famous British ballerina in the world. With her poise and grace, her artistry and skill, Fonteyn represented to balletomanes and the general public alike what a ballerina should look like: elegant, well-dressed, with superb deportment, and often seen carrying a large bouquet of flowers, having just given the most wonderful performance. This is how Fonteyn appeared in a photograph taken during the Sadler's Wells Ballet's tour of North America in 1949. It was this tour that rocketed her to international stardom. Her performance as Aurora in *The Sleeping Beauty*[2] on the opening night of the tour in New York received thunderous applause and countless curtain calls. In the photograph she wears a finely plaited straw hat trimmed with pleated black Petersham ribbon, by Christian Dior.[3]

Throughout her career, Fonteyn was the consummate performer, presenting different characters year after year on the world's stages and also via the new medium of television. Simultaneously, she performed significant offstage roles: home-grown dancer rising to stardom in the emerging British ballet in the 1930s; advocate for British fashion during and after World War II in the 1940s; ballet royalty and ambassador's wife in the 1950s; devoted caregiver and "thoroughly modern miss"[4] in the 1960s. Fonteyn's name changes give a clue to her chameleon-like ability to re-focus herself and take on different personas, in both the public realm and her private life.[5]

One of the key tools that Fonteyn used to effect these role changes was fashion. The concept of becoming a character, of using every available prop to create and sustain that illusion, was, of course, second nature to the ballerina. But she embraced fashion, and the extended world of fashion, in a disciplined way to maintain whatever offstage role she was performing at the time. A letter she wrote to Harry W. Yoxall (1896–1984), managing editor of British *Vogue*, underscores how important the medium of fashion was to her: "I will be back in London on March 18th. Is this too late for you? I do hope not as I should very much like to be photographed for *Vogue*."[6]

Over the course of her career Fonteyn developed a keen awareness of how the clothes that she chose to wear could help to create the persona that the viewer expected to see. Ballet dancer and designer William Chappell (1907–1994) was well aware of this: "Social occasions . . . almost become performances. The dancer is watched closely, from every angle. Stared at, quizzed, and curiously examined, it is obvious how carefully she should present herself when she is to be studied at such close range by her public. The entire responsibility rests on her."[7]

Fonteyn was acutely conscious of how dress could convey messages to her audience—whether adoring fans waiting for a glimpse of the ballerina at the stage door, the world's press assembled on the tarmac for her descent from an aircraft, or guests at an ambassador's dinner—and of how her choice of attire assisted her as a performer to make the audience believe in her, at that moment, in that particular role: "Theatre is, obviously, what I care about and . . . I try to follow the laws of 'theatre' in the field of ballet. These laws are very clear in my mind. First, the audience is always right. . . . Every performance carries a burden of responsibility, and the performer must strive to match the expectations of his public."[8]

Fonteyn followed the same "laws of theatre" in her choice of fashion. Understanding the language of her fashion choices is key to understanding her offstage performances throughout her life.

MODEL AND MANNEQUIN

"Dear Mr Yoxall . . . I should very much
like to be photographed for Vogue."

Margot Fonteyn had already made an impression as a rising star of the Vic-Wells Ballet by the mid-1930s. She was noted in *Façade*,[9] which premiered at Sadler's Wells Theatre in September 1935: "16-year-old Dancer is a Discovery. She is a find, an alert dancer and a smart mimist."[10]

PRECEDING PAGES: Sadler's Wells prima ballerina Margot Fonteyn in a silk brocade evening dress by London-based designer Bianca Mosca, 1949.

Fonteyn's road to prima ballerina assoluta began when, as four-year-old Peggy Hookham, she took dancing lessons, first in London and then in Shanghai, when her family moved to China. She returned to England with her mother and enrolled in the Vic-Wells Ballet School,[11] founded by Ninette de Valois (1898–2008). Fonteyn's mother, Hilda Hookham (1894–1988),[12] was a key figure throughout Fonteyn's career and frequently mentioned in the press: "Mrs Hookham has spent the past 18 months with her daughter. They have a flat in London, and all the time of both mother and daughter seems spent in directing the young lady's career."[13]

Fonteyn was open to influence and good at taking direction. Ninette de Valois recognized this quality and used it to groom her for the role of leading British ballerina, a distinction that she felt the company needed. Onstage, Fonteyn was something of a shapeshifter, capable of transforming herself for each role that she danced. This ability was also evident in her approach to fashion from the late 1930s on, with her uncanny knack for adapting her dress to her offstage roles.

The ballerina's first headline appearance for the Vic-Wells was in *Giselle* in January 1937. That same month she was also featured in the British society magazine *The Sketch*: "Our portrait of Miss Fonteyn shows her wearing a hat adorned with a huge ring, just like those used to tie boats up."[14] Thus, right at the beginning of her public career Margot Fonteyn was identified both as a ballerina and, in effect, as a fashion model, a combination that was to become more pronounced in the 1940s.[15]

Later that year, Margot Fonteyn again appeared modeling fashions of the day, this time in British *Vogue* with fellow Vic-Wells dancers. But though the ballerina's gown, an "off-white quilted satin by Tinling,"[16] is shown to great advantage, the title of the feature and the balletic composition of the images indicate that the emphasis of the story was more on ballet than on fashion.

Ballet was the focus of the story again in 1941, when Fonteyn was photographed for British *Vogue* being fitted with her costume for a new ballet, *Orpheus and Eurydice*. The feature was about the costume designer Matilda Etches (1898–1974): "Dressing a New Ballet. Vic-Wells Dancers

in Matilda Etches' Studio."[17] But as World War II wore on, British *Vogue's* depiction of Fonteyn shifted subtly from ballerina to model/mannequin. In 1944 Fonteyn again appeared in the magazine wearing a garment by Matilda Etches, but this time the focus was on Etches as a fashion designer, rather than as a costumier. The ballerina is attired in a gray flannel dress: "Her dress is simple, closely moulded to her taut dancer's figure."[18] Gone are the theatrical poses; Fonteyn stands in a hallway, a domestic setting with which the magazine's readers could identify. The aim was to raise awareness and generate sales of British fashions, all part of the war effort.

Fonteyn wears a hat by Aage Thaarup (1906–1987) in this photograph. Hats were not subject to the same stringent rationing as other clothing and textiles in Britain during the war, and it is noticeable how frequently hats appear in British *Vogue* in those years. Later that year, Fonteyn again modeled hats by Thaarup for the magazine: "Margot Fonteyn draws her dark hair off her brow, ballerina style." In both articles, Fonteyn is identified as a ballerina but not *shown* as one; instead, she has assumed the role of fashion mannequin showcasing British clothing and accessories.

The ballerina also modeled "vintage" fashions (historical dress from Doris Langley Moore's collection) in a feature giving "make do and mend" tips to readers of British *Vogue* during the dark days of the war:

> Her enchanting jacket with fluted basque was
> made about the turn of the century by the great
> Worth; came into the fine costume collection of Mrs
> Doris Langley Moore (who wrote the scenario for
> the Sadler's Wells new ballet *The Quest*) and was
> given by her to Miss Fonteyn who loves to wear it,
> unaltered, in the evening.... a precious museum
> piece in currency once more, to the great enrichment
> of these austere days.... If *you* are inclined to pilfer
> from the past, only wear unaltered, things whose
> basic line the present-day eye approves.[19]

Through the war years, Fonteyn's appearances in British *Vogue* as a fashion model presenting British fashions, was one of the ways she supported the war effort.

COMPLETE COSMOPOLITAN

"The Maison Dior decided to take me under its wing."

In 1948 Margot Fonteyn took a hiatus from her role as princi-pal ballerina of the Sadler's Wells Company and went to Paris to dance with Roland Petit's (1924–2011) new ballet com-pany. Petit created a role especially for her in his ballet *Les Demoiselles de la Nuit*.[20] He also directed her to a new fashion house in Paris, as she recalled in her autobiography: "He said, 'There's a marvellous new couturier who has just shown his first collection. It's a sensational success. He's called Christian Dior.' He took me to Dior, where they lent me a striking dress to wear that evening. Everyone complimented me on the gown, and I had never felt so elegant in my life."

Christian Dior's first collection, famously christened the "New Look" by Carmel Snow, fashion editor of American *Harper's Bazaar*, was a transformative moment in twentieth-century fashion history. Fonteyn bought one of the New Look ensembles : "The Maison Dior decided to take me under its wing, and I bought one of the first season's outfits. It was called *Daisy*. It was the New Look line, with small waist, nar-row shoulders and bell-shaped skirt to the calf, in complete contrast to the unfeminine war and post-war styles of short, straight skirts and padded military shoulder."[21]

She also acquired a "Goemon" coat from Dior's second New Look collection, shown in July 1947. The coat has the same rounded shoulders, tight-fitting waist, and padding to create the distinctive New Look shape over the hips; it fastens with a row of domed black buttons.[22]

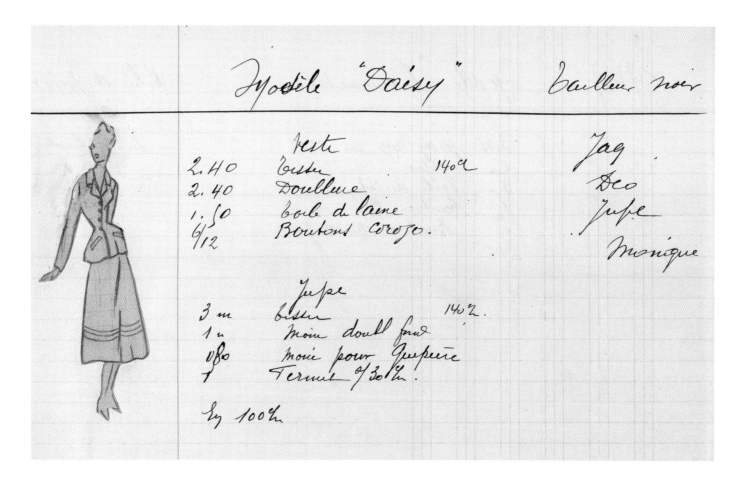

ABOVE: Sketch of the "Daisy" New Look wool suit from the Christian Dior, spring/summer 1947, production ledger.
OPPOSITE: Margot Fonteyn's "Daisy" suit.

Fonteyn's relationship with the Paris couture house gave her a cosmopolitan elegance that was quite different from British fashion. She ordered a number of ensembles from Dior in 1948, including garments from the "Fadette," "Florestan," "Picadilly," and "Sourire" lines.

Was Fonteyn fulfilling a role as "brand ambassador" for Dior during the early years of the house? Given the house's commercial sense, it does not seem unlikely. She was certainly photographed holding a Dior paper advertising fan on the corner of the rue François 1er, close to the couture house's premises.[23] It is noticeable, too, how frequently Christian Dior is named in magazine articles about the ballerina:

> The last two years have brought about a complete
> metamorphosis in the ballerina. A perfectionist down
> to the last detail, it seems that little Miss Hookham,
> having reached a standard of near-perfection in her life's
> work, took stock of herself and emerged the complete
> cosmopolitan. In frequent trips to Paris she learned
> about clothes and discovered that Christian Dior was
> the man she wanted to dress her in private life.[24]

A contact sheet of photographs from the late 1940s shows Fonteyn wearing an elegant, dark-colored suit jacket, which could be the "Daisy," as she tries on hats at British milliner Vernier. The photographer was Elsbeth Juda (1911–2014), who, with her husband, Hans (1904–1975), ran *The Ambassador*, the British export magazine for textiles and fashion.[25] They would become key figures in the next chapter of Fonteyn's sartorial story.

> For although she was now closely aligned with Dior,
> she was soon to play a new role, as an ambassador
> for British fashion on an overseas tour: "I love good
> clothes," Fonteyn told me, hugging herself at the
> thought of the new outfits she had been given for the
> American tour. "Most of my things lately have come
> from Christian Dior. These new ones for New York are,
> of course, by British designers." With her piquant face,
> perfect figure, and beautiful carriage, she is a perfect
> model for the sophisticated clothes she loves.[26]

FASHION AMBASSADOR

*"Her dresses at informal parties and receptions
will be a show window for Britain."*[27]

In September 1949, the Sadler's Wells Ballet embarked on their first tour of North America.[28] A key figure in bringing the company across the Atlantic was the impresario Sol Hurok (1888–1974), a presenter of dance and dancers. The rationale for the tour was Britain's postwar need to earn money through export, primarily through ticket sales; but it was also a unique opportunity to promote British fashion. Hans Juda was credited with the idea that "these dancers would make good 'export mannequins,'"[29] and he approached the Incorporated Society of London Fashion Designers[30] with a proposal that was well received:

> After discussion it was agreed that the proposition
> merited careful consideration. . . . A first impression
> was that each member should supply one model,
> either travel or cocktails, and it would be arranged
> that each of the five Ballerinas—Margot Fonteyn,
> Moira Shearer, Violetta Elvin, Beryl Gray [*sic*], and
> Pamela May would – 1) arrive in the travel model, 2)
> wear the cocktail model at [evening receptions].[31]

The matter of which designer would dress which ballerina would be decided by "drawing names out of a hat."[32] At the Incorporated Society's next meeting, the issue was settled:

> It was agreed that the members (except Captain
> Molyneux and Madame Bianca Mosca who had
> not given a decision) would between them provide
> a travel model and either an evening or a cocktail
> model for each of the five ballerinas. . . . After
> balloting, the draw was. TRAVEL: Amies—~~Violetta
> Elvin~~[33] Ninette de Valois, Creed—Pamela May,
> Sherard—Margot Fonteyn, Mattli—Moira Shearer,
> Stiebel—Beryl Grey; EVENING: Hartnell—Beryl
> Grey, Bianca Mosca—Margot Fonteyn, Digby
> Morton—Moira Shearer, Russell—~~Violetta Elvin~~

Evening dress by Christian Dior, ca. 1948, worn by Margot Fonteyn.

Ninette de Valois, Worth—Pamela May. The Secretary was asked to ascertain from Mr Webster[34] of Covent Garden which was going to be the most important function of the tour—a cocktail party or an evening dress function. Depending upon his answers each of the five Members would provide either a cocktail or an evening dress.[35]

The making of the ballerinas' on-tour wardrobe was widely reported in Britain. It was of particular interest to regional newspapers in textile- and clothing-producing areas such as Yorkshire, where woolen cloth was made. Margot Fonteyn headlined many of the articles:[36]

> Margot Fonteyn, Britain's prima ballerina, in preparation for her dollar-earning tour of America and Canada with the Sadler's Wells Ballet Company, achieved every girl's dream. She watched a dress collection of fifty-three suits, overcoats, afternoon and evening dresses costing between 60 and 100 guineas, knowing she could choose anything she liked for herself, for nothing. . . . Miss Fonteyn's choice for travel was a suit and coat[37] in thunder-blue and black Yorkshire herringbone suiting.[38]

After arriving in New York, Fonteyn was photographed in a gray worsted jacket and pleated skirt ensemble by Hardy Amies[39] She had already been seen in this suit in the UK,[40] and it had been featured in American *Vogue* the previous year: "Hardy Amies ticket to anywhere suit, for here, there, and en route, of Yorkshire worsted. A round-at-the-edges jacket, taffeta-lined pleated skirt. Available at Henri Bendel, Marshall Field, I. Magnin, Hudson's"[41]

The Hardy Amies suit was clearly a favorite; Fonteyn was photographed wearing it at a down-time party at J. Talbot Hughes's mansion.[42] At more formal occasions, however, the ballerina wore the black wool suit by Michael Sherard that she had been given for "travel." She also wore the suit at a cocktail party hosted by Hans Juda. The invitation read in part: ". . . to meet the Ballerinas and Corps de Ballet of the Sadler's Wells Company from the Royal Opera House, Covent Garden London at the Metropolitan Opera House New York (Louis Sherry Buffet and Restaurant, Grand Tier Floor) on Friday October 7 at 4.30.[43]

American fashion retailers had been invited, with the aim of generating orders for the designs of the British couturiers. Influential fashion editor Carmel Snow of *Harper's Bazaar* and fashion designers Claire McCardell and Jacques Fath were also on the guest list.

The Sadler's Wells four principal dancers—Beryl Grey, Margot Fonteyn, Pamela May, and Moira Shearer—had also been featured in British *Vogue*[44] wearing the evening dresses that the British couturiers had designed for them. Cecil Beaton photographed Fonteyn wearing the black flower-patterned silk two-piece evening gown—a strapless bodice with a bow at the front and a three-tiered, flounced skirt—designed for her by Bianca Mosca.[45]

Two days after the cocktail party, following her triumphant performance in *The Sleeping Beauty*, Fonteyn again wore the Bianca Mosca gown at an evening reception given by the mayor of New York at Gracie Mansion. The company was celebrated and feted, and its star ballerina became the toast of the town:

> Fine Margot! You're the talk
> Of all New York!
> Notably you have added fame
> To Britain's name!
> Even though Broadway's strewn with "flops"
> Yours is genuine, nothing stops;
> New York proclaims it—you're the "tops"![46]

Fonteyn appeared on the cover of *Time* magazine, the ultimate accolade, with a feature inside on the economic success of the tour:

> Five weeks ago, when the Sadler's Wells Company of 65 bundled into two Constellations bound for New York, the dancers were weighted down with uncertainty. It was costing $50,000 to bring them on their first visit to the US, a place where ballet, while spreading to every nightclub and skating

Worsted wool suit by Hardy Amies, 1948, worn by Margot Fonteyn.

OPPOSITE AND ABOVE: Silk brocade evening dress by Bianca Mosca, 1949, worn by Margot Fonteyn.

rink, had lost much of its popular appeal and much of its professional standing. The British Council, which would be called on to make up any losses, had bid them god speed with the air of men watching $50,000 or more go up in smoke. . . . Night after night the Met was packed to the fire-limit (for an all-time record ballet box-office gross of $256,000). In four weeks, Margot Fonteyn and Sadler's Wells had restored as much glitter to Britain's tarnished tiara as any mission the English had sent abroad since the war. . . . Her perfectly proportioned ballerina body, her effortless grace and technique, had US ballet connoisseurs and critics going back for comparisons to such ballet immortals as Anna Pavlova, Olga Spessivtzeva and Tamara Karsavina, the sometime partner of the great Nijinsky."[47]

In addition to "restoring glitter to Britain's tarnished tiara" by publicly wearing the supplied travel and evening clothes, Fonteyn wore fashions by Christian Dior during the 1949 tour. A description of one dress, "Marigny,"[48] is included in the article "Swan Queen Shops," describing how Fonteyn and colleague Robert Helpmann (1909–1986) had delighted in visiting a self-serve grocery store in Washington, D.C.:

> Miss Fonteyn possesses, incidentally, the most enviable wardrobe. At an after-theatre supper given for the ballet company at the British Embassy, she wore a cream-coloured satin Dior dress. Buttoned high at her miniscule [sic] waist, the highly swathed skirt cascaded in off-side panels to for a train. The jacket, impractical but enchanting, was single-sleeved, embroidered with dangling crystal beads and tied with double satin streamer to the opposite shoulder strap.[49]

The Sadler's Wells Ballet's tour of North America in 1949 was such a success[50] that it was the Chancellor of the Exchequer, Sir Stafford Cripps, who welcomed the company home at Covent Garden. "You have no idea what pride it aroused in the fastness of Treasury chambers to discover that to their

ABOVE: "Marigny" satin evening dress by Christian Dior, spring/summer 1949, worn by Margot Fonteyn.
OPPOSITE: Detail of the "Marigny" satin jacket with sequins and dangling crystal beads by Christian Dior, spring/summer 1949.

other outstanding qualities Sadler's Wells was added that of the dollar earner,"[51] he told them, adding: "They are lasting ties that you have woven, which will draw us all still closer to our friends on the other side of the Atlantic."[52]

The gamble of the company's tour, on a scale never undertaken before, underpinned by the British government, to present not only British culture but also British fashion as export commodities, had paid off. And Margot Fonteyn had played a starring role in both endeavors.

BRITAIN'S STAR BALLERINA

"... an international figure, a balletic royalty"[53]

After the ballerina returned in triumph from the 1949 North American tour, her presence at theater premieres and other events was widely reported. In January 1950, for example, she was photographed wearing the black, tiered Bianca Mosca gown at the premiere of Christopher Fry's play *Venus Observed* at St James's Theatre, accompanied by Robert Helpmann. Her increased visibility on the London social scene at this time was a matter of comment: "The rather hard, serious singleness of purpose that kept her for so long away from the social worlds has softened: nowadays even when she is dancing the next night at the Garden, she *has* been seen, though not very late, having supper, dressed by Dior, and very gay, in fashionable places in the West End."[54]

Although Fonteyn had always been of interest to the press, from the early 1950s on, she was the subject of lengthier "lifestyle" features. As the appetite for more information about a character who had become national property grew, Margot Fonteyn's personal secretary drafted briefing notes: "Likes—Many—including China tea without milk or sugar; masses of flowers; Christian Dior dresses; unlimited pairs of gloves. Relaxations—No hobbies. For relaxation enjoys travelling; swimming; theatre-going."[55]

Again, the ballerina's choice of Dior is noted. A favorite dress was "Debussy," an evening ensemble in blue silk net embroidered with iridescent sequins, featuring a strapless

bodice, slender column-like skirt, and separate sweeping train, from Dior's Ligne Verticale collection.[56]

Client books show that Fonteyn ordered extensively at Christian Dior in autumn 1951. Her purchases included an "Aristide" dress and jacket, a "Monaco" dress and coat, an "Oscar" suit, a "Paraguay" cocktail dress, and an "Australie" evening dress in black silk taffeta.

Fonteyn's national status was officially confirmed when she was awarded a CBE in the Birthday Honours of 1951; she received the decoration at an investiture in Buckingham Palace in October of that year. In 1954 she was elected presi-

OPPOSITE: "Debussy" evening dress by Christian Dior, spring/summer 1950, worn by Margot Fonteyn.
ABOVE: Press sketch of the "Debussy" evening dress, spring/summer 1950, Ligne Verticale collection.

dent of the Royal Academy of Dance,[57] a position she held for the rest of her life. Images show her wearing Dior when she accepted both of these honors.

British magazines commented frequently on the fact that Fonteyn was not married: "At 33, this vivid dancer, half English, half Brazilian, has no hobbies and no husband. There is only dancing in her life. . . . Beautiful clothes, drinking champagne, enjoying good food, the theatre, opera and jitter-bugging are some of the things Margot relishes when not thinking about dancing."[58]

The comments ceased, however, in February 1955, when she married Dr. Roberto de Arias (1918–1989)[59] at the Panamanian Consulate in Paris. Fonteyn chose a silver-gray silk taffeta dress with a draped bodice by Christian Dior for her wedding dress, pairing it with a headdress incorporating vivid turquoise feathers.

Shortly after the wedding, de Arias was named the Panamanian ambassador to the Court of St James, and Fonteyn took on a new role: ambassador's wife, one of the main functions of which was entertaining foreign dignitaries. A series of dinner books from the mid-1950s provides listings of the guests, seating arrangements, and menus at these events. On March 22, 1955, for example, Fonteyn and de Arias entertained the ambassador of the Republic of the Philippines to the United Kingdom, Léon Maria Guerro III, at the Savoy Hotel Grill, following a performance of *Firebird*.[60] Fonteyn used the "Remarques" section in the dinner books to note what she wore on each occasion, in this case: "Dark blue long dress."

By 1955, Fonteyn had taken on two new high-profile roles. In addition to becoming the wife of the Panamanian ambassador, she was made a DBE in the New Year Honours of 1955. Henceforth, she was known as Dame Margot Fonteyn de Arias. That spring, she ordered more Dior creations, including an "Aioli" dress, an "Anglomanie" dress and jacket, and an "Aragonaise" evening dress.

Fonteyn's appointment diaries from the 1950s indicate that she flew regularly to Paris for fittings at Dior—generally arriving in the afternoon and returning to London in the evening—but she also visited the British couturiers of the Incorporated Society of London Fashion Designers, including

Victor Stiebel in February 1958 and John Cavanagh in October 1959. And she went to the British ready-to-wear firms of the Fashion House Group of London, including Horrockses Fashions[61] and Susan Small.[62]

Airports and aircraft steps served as key theatrical spaces for Fonteyn in her offstage roles throughout her career. But one particular image of her emerging from an aircraft was especially dramatic. In 1959 Arias attempted to overthrow the

OPPOSITE: Margot Fonteyn wears a silver-gray silk taffeta Christian Dior dress on her wedding day, February 1955.
ABOVE: Margot Fonteyn and her husband, Dr. Roberto de Arias, on their wedding day.

Panamanian government, and Fonteyn, whether knowingly or unknowingly, figured in the plot: " Dame Margot Fonteyn, Britain's star ballerina, was being held as a hostage in Panama City's cockroach-infested gaol last night."[63]

The world's press was awaiting Fonteyn when she arrived back in Britain after her release from custody.[64] The role that she assumed was that of the innocent, the wrongly imprisoned. It was pure theater, with the aircraft door the equivalent of the wings from which the performer makes her entrance, the aircraft steps the stage, and the audience, anxious for a glimpse of the ballerina, amassed not in the stalls but on the airport tarmac. The gaze of the world was upon her and she played the role to perfection: ". . . wearing a white woollen coat of stylish cut, she was the essence of chic."[65] Although Fonteyn's ensemble was not identified, the light-colored, loose-fitting coat has the hallmarks of Paris couture, possibly from Yves Saint Laurent's first collection for Dior, Trapeze. The indelible impression of Britain's star ballerina, unjustly accused, was created through the elegance of couture—and an oversized bouquet of flowers.

THE AMAZING MARGOT FONTEYN

". . . and is still counted among the
world's best-dressed women."

That same year, 1959, Fonteyn turned forty, and there was speculation about the ballerina's retirement. But in 1961 two unconnected events in Paris changed both her ballet career and her fashion look. The young Soviet dancer Rudolph Nureyev (1938–1993) defected during the Kirov Ballet's tour to the West, and Yves Saint Laurent, previously chief designer at Christian Dior, opened his own couture house. Both events proved transformational for Fonteyn, causing her to take on new roles and reinvent herself yet again.

Ninette de Valois suggested to Fonteyn that she dance with Nureyev: "De Valois told me that Rudolf would dance *Giselle* at Covent Garden in February, three months ahead. 'Do you want to do it with him?' she asked. My immediate reaction was to say, 'Oh my goodness! I think it would be like mutton dancing with lamb. Don't you think I'm too old?'"[66]

Heeding de Valois's advice, Fonteyn overcame her reservations about the age disparity, and in February 1962 she and Nureyev danced together in *Giselle*,[67] to rapturous applause and rave reviews:

> The ballerina curtsies to the public with all the
> humble grace which comes so naturally to her, then
> she presents a rose from her bouquet to the boy who
> up to this point has been looking rather dazed. In a
> gesture that appears to be spontaneous the boy sinks
> to one knee, grasps the ballerina's hand and covers
> it with kisses. . . . when Nureyev kneeled to kiss the
> hand that offered him the rose it could have been
> a gesture that, unbeknown to anyone at the time,
> heralded a new ballet boom for Britain.[68]

The partnership gave Fonteyn a new lease on life that extended to the way she dressed. She had continued to order clothes from Dior after Christian Dior's death in 1957, when Yves Saint Laurent took over as chief designer. And she stayed with Saint Laurent when he opened his own house and found his own creative language, innovatively applying the traditions of Paris couture to the "Youthquake" trend in fashion.

Fonteyn's look changed dramatically during the mid-1960s, and images from this time—dancing in a nightclub in New York with Nureyev, for example—show how she embraced the new styles, including shift dresses and the mini-skirt length. "And with characteristic gaiety, she audaciously wears St Laurent creations for the 'modern miss,' complete with above-knee skirts."[69]

Fonteyn was dancing with Nureyev at the Bath Festival in 1964 when the shocking news reached her that her husband had been shot in Panama City. She danced on, but then flew to his bedside, eventually accompanying him back to the U.K. for treatment. On her return, she wore a navy blue straw pillbox style hat by Yves Saint Laurent.[70] The assassination attempt left Arias a quadriplegic and in need of full-time care for the rest of his life. It was a role that Fonteyn embraced, and newspaper images and articles chronicled her love and devotion.

Margot Fonteyn in an Yves Saint Laurent ostrich feather cocktail dress with Rudolf Nureyev at a discotheque in New York, 1965.

ABOVE: Ostrich feather cocktail dress and coat by Yves Saint Laurent, 1965, worn by Margot Fonteyn.
OPPOSITE: Detail of the rhinestone ornamentation on the ostrich feather cocktail dress by Yves Saint Laurent, 1965.

Fonteyn wore Yves Saint Laurent throughout the 1960s, including a white silk gauze dress with sequin embroidery in a zigzag design,[71] seen in a photograph with her ballet teacher Tamara Karsavina (1885–1978). If Dior's name was connected with her in the late 1940s and until his death in 1957, Yves Saint Laurent was the name most closely associated with her in the 1960s: "Yves Saint Laurent, Margot Fonteyn's favourite couturier," and ". . . Yves Saint Laurent, from whom she buys most of her clothes."[72]

In 1965, before she and Nureyev embarked on a tour of Australia, the modernity of her dress was noted at a reception at the Café Royal in London: "Britain's *prima ballerina assoluta*, Dame Margot Fonteyn, appeared in a dramatic confrontation of opposites—black and white, mink and plastic—as a sort of spirit of Op Art."[73]

The dress that she wore was Saint Laurent's "Mondrian," a cream wool jersey shift with a navy blue "cross" feature,[74] one of the most acclaimed styles in twentieth-century fashion history (see page 200). That the most famous ballerina in the world wore the most famous fashions in the world—Christian Dior's New Look and Yves Saint Laurent's "Mondrian" dress—underscores her status as a leading exponent and advocate not only of the finest ballet in the world but also of the finest fashion in the mid-twentieth century.

THE COMPLETE PROFESSIONAL

"A performer of incomparable grace,
imagination and charm, she made
the ballet more fashionable than it had
ever been since Diaghilev, and more
accessible than it had ever been."[75]

Margot Fonteyn is still spoken of as the greatest dancer of her generation, a ballerina with superb line, excellent technique, superlative acting skills, great sensitivity to music, grace, passion, and discipline. As colleague Anthony Dowell (b. 1943) noted: "She was always the complete professional. . . . But she also behaved beautifully on the other side of the footlights. . . . It was always a faultless performance, on and off stage."[76]

Above all, Fonteyn was a performer and believed that she must always be in character: "Every performance carries a burden of responsibility, and the performer must strive to match the expectations of his public." She was acutely conscious of her image, and she used her clothes to establish it. Her wardrobe choices saw her through the progression of roles that she performed off the stage from the 1930s through the 1960s, helping not only her audience but also Fonteyn herself to believe in who she was.

OPPOSITE: Sequined silk gauze mini-dress by Yves Saint Laurent, 1966.
ABOVE: Margot Fonteyn wearing the Yves Saint Laurent mini-dress with former prima ballerina of the Ballets Russes Tamara Karsavina, 1966.

DRYADS OF WEST 55TH STREET

JOEL LOBENTHAL

The curtain was always up: offstage during the 1950s, ballerinas of New York City Ballet (NYCB) employed sartorial strategies designed to sustain theatrical illusion. They costumed themselves as exponents of a chic and an allure distinct from but coextensive with their balletic identities. They reprimanded junior members of the company whose attire they considered careless or dowdy. For the ballerinas, sloppiness was a mark of disrespect for the art form, a betrayal of the dancer's obligation to it and to her public.

Engaged in a landmark Americanization of ballet, they nevertheless were molded by Euro-Russian traditions. The roster of NYCB, founded by George Balanchine and Lincoln Kirstein in 1948, drew heavily on American veterans of the Ballet Russe de Monte Carlo, which was one of a number of companies that sprang up in the wake of Sergei Diaghilev's death in 1929. They perpetuated the legacy of his émigré Ballets Russes. Stranded in America during World War II, Ballet Russe crisscrossed the country on tours that lasted for months, visiting scores of large and small American cities.

Recalling NYCB prima ballerina Maria Tallchief, colleague Robert Barnett said, "When Maria left the theater you knew you were looking at somebody. Maria never left when she wasn't done to the nines. She learned that from Danilova."[1] Alexandra Danilova was Ballet Russe prima ballerina when Tallchief joined that company in 1942. Before the public, the older ballerina invariably presented an image of invincible, indefatigable ebullience and glamour. Thirty years earlier, she had entered the state ballet academy in tsarist St. Petersburg. Many of the female dancers in Russian ballet companies occupied prominent positions in haute bourgeois, even quasi-aristocratic circles. It was probably with that precedent in mind that Danilova tutored, prodded, and all but policed the younger American women in Ballet Russe to follow her lead.

Visiting Europe during the 1950s helped NYCB position itself amid an international cultural pantheon. The tours were subsidized in part by the U.S. State Department, which appreciated the company's efficacy as cultural ambassadors. After its British debut in 1950, British critic Arnold Haskell wrote that NYCB had done more "for the artistic prestige" of the U.S. "than a carload of crooners, ten years' run

of musicals, a high powered comedian and a million reels of Hollywood celluloid all added together."[2]

"We were representing America," NYCB's Barbara Walczak recalls.[3] On tour, the dancers were frequently invited to important social and diplomatic functions. When NYCB prepared for its first European tour in 1952, an assortment of Seventh Avenue wholesale firms provided a special outfit for each woman in the company. *Look* magazine photographed the dancers in their new clothes.

Ballet's expanding popularity and visibility were enhanced by the fashion world's infatuation with balletic costume design: voluminous, diaphanous skirts, the second-skin silhouette with some stretch added to the fabric. But in certain respects ballet costumes served as a refutation of some of the era's more restrictive fashion carapaces.

Then growing up in a suburb of Los Angeles, Linda Gravenites would, a decade later, make clothes for musicians in Haight-Ashbury, San Francisco, ground zero for the explosion of riotous street costumes in the 1960s. As a teenager, Gravenites dreamed of designing ballet costumes, which attracted her because "[t]hey weren't bound to reality—they're quintessential. They can be breathtakingly beautiful and strange and yet they must also be utterly functional." For her, "they were the antithesis of the push-'em-up bras and the waist cinches and everything we were armored in" during the 1950s.[4]

Popular entertainment's interest in balletic talent also kept the art form prominent in America's consciousness. As a girl, NYCB's Tanaquil Le Clercq had been offered a long-term Paramount contract. As adults, Tallchief, Diana Adams, Melissa Hayden, Allegra Kent, Nora Kaye, and Janet Reed each danced on Broadway and/or in Hollywood feature films. The most exotic, enticing, but forbidding of the performing arts, ballet now found itself simultaneously saluted and subjected to normalization by mainstream American media. "Practically Anybody Can Be a Ballet Dancer" is hardly a true statement, but it was the headline of an article that appeared under Le Clercq's byline in *Good Housekeeping* in 1955. Thus NYCB's ballerinas became icons of mass as well as esoteric culture.

PRECEDING PAGES: NYCB ballerina Tanaquil Le Clercq shopping at Capezio. *Cosmopolitan*, 1952.
OPPOSITE, FROM LEFT TO RIGHT: NYCB ballerinas Melissa Hayden, Maria Tallchief, and Tanaquil Le Clercq in Paris, 1955.

Tallchief was an expert needlewoman; her Ballet Russe colleague Nora White recalled going to buy fabric from which each was going to make a dress. Balanchine was at that moment married to Tallchief and he "pinned them on us the way he thought it should kind of look."[5]

Whether he was romantically interested in a woman or not, his artistic control encompassed the proprietary. NYCB ballerina Patricia Wilde recalled arriving at the company's rehearsal studios after tying the nuptial knot at City Hall that same morning. She was beset with colleagues peppering her with the rather anxious query, "Does Mr. B know?"[6]

At mid-century it was NYCB ballerina Le Clercq who best exemplified the aspects of ballet that were influencing popular entertainment and fashion. She epitomized the sleekness, elegance, and elongation that ballet has always projected. And it was she who most emblematically traversed the worlds of fashion and ballet. She was frequently seen in the pages of the glossy magazines, both modeling clothes and being chronicled in dance portraiture. Her patrician features comported exactly with the image of contemporary high-fashion models. She also staked out her own identity as a photographer, keeping a darkroom backstage at New York's City Center, NYCB's home theater from its first night in 1948 until it moved to Lincoln Center in 1964.

At the same time she had a quasi-official role: de facto first lady of the company, as well as some type of variant on the trophy wife, by virtue of the fact that in December 1952 she became Balanchine's fifth wife. Her career was as extraordinary as it was brief, curtailed at its height in 1956 when she was stricken with polio.

A few months after NYCB debuted, Jerome Robbins joined the company as both choreographer and dancer. He had been associated with rival Ballet Theatre for the previous decade. It was in part Le Clercq's dancing that inspired him to shift company allegiance. They also became exceedingly close personally and professionally.

At five feet, six-and-a-half inches, Le Clercq was very tall for a ballerina at that time. Her arms and legs were long and thin to the point of exaggeration. Relative scale and

Creating their image—and create it they did—NYCB's ballerinas negotiated a virtual three-way mirror of objectification. Their professional identities hinged on perpetual self-objectification as well as on nightly interaction with the responsive objectification of their audience. Equally important to their careers was their ability to see themselves through the essentially omniscient gaze of artistic director Balanchine. It is rare in ballet for a choreographer or company director to exert so total a jurisdiction over his dancers' development and artistic sensibility.

Forty-four when he started NYCB, Balanchine had already lived more than a lifetime's worth of epochal cultural achievement. He was the quintessential Pygmalion as well as harem pasha.

ABOVE: "Mrs. George Balanchine," *Vogue*, March 1, 1953. OPPOSITE: *Tanaquil Le Clercq*, New York, 1947. Photograph by Irving Penn.

changing visual criteria have always dictated our percep-tions of appearances. It is certainly startling today to read nineteenth-century ballet critics like Théophile Gautier crit-icizing contemporary ballerinas for being scrawny, since until World War I, ballerinas remained for the most part—to our eyes—extremely muscular. Though length and judicious proportion have long been privileged in ballet, at the advent of Le Clercq's career, the field was still welcoming of more var-ied and rounded ballerina physiques. Irina Baronova, star of Ballet Russe and Ballet Theatre, "looked wonderful," her col-league John Taras recalled. "You never thought of her as fat; you thought of her as luscious."[7] But roundness and ripeness were not what Balanchine was after. He valued the way Le Clercq multiplied the possibilities for abstract, archetypal dis-tillation, an ideal toward which ballet has always aspired. And he was aware of the emotional appeal that the slight touch of gawkiness she retained from early in her career could partic-ularly engage the audience.

Le Clercq seemed downright extreme to some. As her teacher Muriel Stuart recalled, "There were many people that didn't like Tanny's dancing at all."[8] But as unique as her appearance was, she to some degree imagined herself as suc-cessor to Diaghilev ballerina Felia Doubrovska, for whom Balanchine had made important roles during the 1920s. In those days, Doubrovska was considered so tall that she was not given conventional supported adagio roles. She was lean, shapely, aloof, and, like Le Clercq, somewhat outré. Doubrovska's husband, Pierre Vladimiroff, had taught at Balanchine's School of American Ballet (SAB) since its incep-tion in 1934, when Doubrovska was still performing. Fifteen years later, she, too, joined the SAB faculty. Watching her, "I really thought this is very chic and very elegant and this is what I would like to look like," Le Clercq recalled. "And I had never seen anybody I *really* wanted to look like. . . . So to see Doubrovska looking so modern was indeed a terrific shock."[9]

"Modern" in Le Clercq's vocabulary we must presume to mean abstract and modernistic. For in Le Clercq's day, as in our own, what we describe as "modern" is more than an acknowledgment of the topical. The Doubrovska-Le Clercq lineage suggested a new frontier of essentialized, post-representational modern art. In 1949 Le Clercq danced with Merce Cunningham and Betty Nichols in a performance of Cunningham's work in Paris. Among those attending was Alberto Giacometti. "People said that *we* were Giacomettis," Nichols recalled.[10]

Onstage and off, Le Clercq presented herself with dis-tinctive flair and discernment. Asked in 1981 for a possible explanation of Tanaquil's particular style, her mother, Edith, recalled that as a girl her daughter liked to watch her sew.[11] Edith "darned all of Tanny's many toe shoes," colleague Pat McBride Lousada recalled, "and knitted her beautiful tights and sweaters and skirts."[12] By the time her daughter was prominent, Edith herself was an elegant, silver-haired doy-enne, frequently accompanying the company when it toured.

Le Clercq "knew what to do with herself," Barnett recalled. In 1951 Robbins choreographed *The Cage*, in which Nora Kaye was cast as an insect whose mating rites prove fatal for her partners. Three years later, Le Clercq took on the role and devised a different look for it. She discarded the helmet-like wig that Kaye had worn and instead "took her hair and braided it and used egg whites to stiffen it like ten-tacles on her head," Barnett recalled. "It was completely her idea." Dancing Odette in Balanchine's one-act *Swan Lake*, "again she did everything her way," Barnett said. And that meant going all the way. She eschewed the customary pink tights for white and opted for pale makeup; "She was white from one end to the other."[13]

"I wish I were very rich and could buy lots of things," Le Clercq wrote to Robbins in 1956.[14] The life of NYCB ballerinas was paradoxical: onstage they were often immersed in fan-tasy and opulence, but offstage, money was tight. City Center was established in 1943 in a former Shriners Temple on West 55th Street with the mandate of making high-level perfor-mance financially accessible to the masses. Ticket prices were considerably lower than they were at the Metropolitan Opera, which was the city's most prestigious venue for dance as well as grand opera. NYCB's dancers were happy to be attracting a new, popular audience to the art form, but salaries were poor. The company existed on a shoestring; backstage staff was skeletal, and ballerinas did their own hair and makeup, assisting each other when needed.

Husbands and family could help: Le Clercq's mother came from a moneyed St. Louis family. But profligacy was a rare event. "I lost my head today," she wrote Robbins from Paris, where NYCB was performing at the Opera. "I spent 27,000 francs on perfume and gloves. I always loose [sic] gloves but these are so adorable with embroidered roses . . . and a flower over each finger tip—and then there is one pair with a tiny blue flower on the index finger." Balanchine's first wife, dancer and actress Tamara Geva, had written asking Le Clercq to buy her an ounce of any perfume of her own choosing. "So I felt generous and got her a tremendous bottle. Oh dear everything looks so good here."

Certainly, the added income fashion modeling could bring was welcome to the young dancer. In September 1951 she was recovering from an ankle injury and couldn't dance in NYCB's City Center season. Her hiatus, however, went to good use. "Got a marvelous modeling job," she wrote Robbins, who was in London. "Vogue-lingerie from 10:00 to 5:00 at night All day long—and so much money." More attention followed. "Vogue sent [me] to the hairdressers to have my hair cut (seems I ain't chic) so am doing lots more modeling with 'me new coifure [sic].'"

Le Clercq was a twenty-year-old star engaged to the Dutch composer Jurien Andriessen when Balanchine began a two-year courtship. In June 1952, during the Paris leg of the company's first European tour, he bought her two evening gowns at Christian Dior. They were most likely model's samples, given that her schedule didn't permit extended fittings, and given that despite his enormous prestige and influence, Balanchine never had very much money. (That year he was even considering becoming a Vespa salesman rather than having to supplement his income by choreographing Broadway shows.) On the flight home in September, Le Clercq stowed one of her Dior gowns in an overhead luggage compartment. She spent much of the flight talking and laughing with company member Michael Maule and forgot to retrieve the gown when she left the plane. By the time she realized the oversight, it was too late—it had been stolen.

Balanchine was "furious," Walczak recalled. "I don't think he ever forgave her."[15] Nevertheless, they were married on New Year's Eve of that year.

"It was perhaps Tanaquil Le Clercq who made plain a kinship between Balanchine's image of women and that of contemporary fashion designers," Deborah Jowitt writes in Time and the Dancing Image.[16] Always on the lookout for heightened artistic impact, Balanchine believed that Le Clercq's striking and vanguard image could be heightened further. Le Clercq had her own apartment by the time she married, but in 1998, toward the end of her life, she recalled the stark contrast between the breakfasts her mother used to prepare for her and those that Balanchine permitted her. Every morning, her mother gave her freshly squeezed orange

New York City Ballet is feted at the American Embassy in Paris, October 1956. George Balanchine is at right.

juice, two four-minute eggs, two pieces of white, crustless, buttered bread, four slices of crispy bacon, and Ovaltine. Balanchine served her strong coffee and a dry zwieback.[17]

Vagaries of funding meant that at NYCB costumes and scenery might be lavish or virtually nonexistent. When Balanchine's *Western Symphony*, a rollicking cowboy romp, premiered in September 1954, there was no money in the budget for costumes. Instead, the dancers wore sweaters over tights; the principals could choose their own colors. Four couples backed up Le Clercq and Jacques d'Amboise in the ballet's closing Rondo. One night the ensemble women decided that they would exchange their brown sweaters for red. But Le Clercq had apparently also had similar thoughts about revising whatever color she'd originally chosen. "That performance, Tanny came down in a red sweater!" Walczak recalled. "We thought we would die. It was too late to change it."[18]

In February 1955, the ballet was reborn on the City Center stage with Wild West backdrop and full costume regalia. Barbara Karinska's costume for Le Clercq included an enormous, plumed fantasia on a cartwheel hat. In *The Nation*, B. H. Haggin declared that her hat, "to say nothing of the way that she wore it, was itself worth the price of admission."[19]

But for Balanchine, necessity could be seen as midwife to aesthetic preference. Minimal costuming for much of the repertory was due not only to economy. Both in Russia and in the West, the young Balanchine had discerned a distinct trend toward streamlining. He instituted further paring away, a privileging of the body in movement over the specific connotations—and sometimes limitations—of costume. Scenery at NYCB was often similarly reduced to a bare cyclorama—usually in an azure blue, a color that had figured prominently in ballet's centuries of moonlight and procession.

Balanchine's *The Four Temperaments* was originally danced in elaborate costumes by surrealist painter Kurt Seligmann. They enclosed Le Clercq and other leading dancers in constructions meant to suggest the medieval humors evoked by Paul Hindemith's score. Before opening night in 1946, however, Balanchine stripped off some of the costumes' excrescences. Several years later, he entirely replaced them

with monochromatic leotards and tights, which soon became a template for much of the repertory, a formalized uniform of sorts, sometimes augmented with short practice skirts for the women. It became as central to the image of contemporary ballet as the tutu was to the classical repertory or the tulle skirt to the Romantic. The spareness and exposure of the new costume protocol meant that bodies like Le Clercq's would be favored.

In Robbins's works, too, the dancers sometimes wore practice clothes, but the attire was less monochromatic and had a less rarefied connotation. His dancers were contemporary personifications of "real" people. In 1936 NYCB co-founder Kirstein had sponsored a small troupe, Ballet Caravan, that was tasked with making ballets on subjects of American vernacular. That was not Balanchine's customary territory at the time; Ballet Caravan depended instead on young American choreographers. Robbins's first choreographic work, *Fancy Free* (1944), was created for Ballet Theatre, but it would have been right at home at Ballet Caravan.

A ballet somewhat in that tradition at NYCB was *Jones Beach* (1950), a collaboration between Balanchine and Robbins. Le Clercq, Tallchief, and Hayden, as well as their male partners, wore Jantzen bathing suits in a series of vignettes that were by turns romantic, humorous, and festive.

Often in Robbins's work the dancers appeared as theatrical projections of themselves. In *The Pied Piper* (1951), they purported to be performers hypnotized by an onstage clarinetist playing Aaron Copland's Clarinet Concerto. In the pursuit of verisimilitude, they were encouraged to wear their own practice clothes: "We even got paid for providing our own 'costumes,'" Le Clercq recalled in 1974.[20] For a *Cosmopolitan* magazine profile in the fall of 1952, she was photographed unpacking a trunk, wearing the same striped leotard she had worn onstage in *The Pied Piper* across Europe that past summer.

Although Balanchine was the company's supreme Pygmalion, he was by no means its only one. As in the fashion world, men were influential advisers and arbiters, directing the way that women should look. Some of the company men were

Tanaquil Le Clercq (foreground) and members of New York City Ballet dance Jerome Robbins's *The Pied Piper*, 1953.

themselves fashion plates. "Roy and Nicky set the tone," principal dancer Jonathan Watts recalled of fellow principals Roy Tobias and Nicholas Magallanes. "Roy was enamored with Savile Row," Watts said. "Special English shoe boots."[21]

From Munich, Le Clercq wrote to Robbins in 1956: "I got a beautiful Italian sweater it has a square collar that goes over your head and ties on top, making a hat—it's white Roy urged me to buy it, and now he tells me I look like a milk bottle."

NYCB dancer Janice Cohen recalled strolling through Venice with colleague Herbert Bliss, a close platonic pal. They stopped in front of a shop window featuring a mannequin in a gray knit dress. "Herbie said, 'You know, you would look beautiful in that dress. Go and try it on.'" It was way beyond her means but she agreed to humor him. "'What about those high heels? Try it with those high heels. . . . Sling that purse over your shoulder.'" After she'd changed back into her own clothes and they continued on their way, she noticed that Bliss was carrying a shopping bag containing, she soon discovered, "'everything you looked so beautiful in.'"[22]

"I used to be a shopper for Maria," Barnett recalled wryly. He had originally studied fashion design. On tour, the dancers received a daily expense allotment in local currency. Tallchief's often went unused, "because everybody was always taking her out to dinner," Barnett said. "When we were in Rome once, she says, 'Bobby, I have a pile of all this lira and I don't know what to do with it. Why don't you go out and go shopping for me?' So I went down to where all the nice shops were and bought her a brooch. I saw her several years ago," Barnett recounted in 2011, "and she still had it."[23]

NYCB's eclectic repertory allowed its members to inhabit a balletic cosmos that ranged across time and space. Reverberations of the past informed new incarnations of enduring archetypes. Robbins's *Afternoon of a Faun* (1953) used the same Debussy score as Vaslav Nijinsky had used for his version in 1912. But whereas Nijinsky's *Faun* was set in a pagan woodland, Robbins transplanted it to an American ballet studio. As she had in *The Pied Piper*, Le Clercq impersonated a contemporary dancer; she studied her mirrored reflection as much as she acknowledged the palpable existence of the male body supporting her. For her, Irene Sharaff designed a tunic that suggested a contemporary woman's one-piece bathing suit or a dancer's practice outfit, but also retained an allusion to the tunics of the archaic Aegean. Her shoulder-length hair was loose, rather than confined in the classical chignon. Epochs conflated and merged; millennia of mythical allure were distilled. She was described in this ballet as "a dryad of Fifth Avenue."[24]

In Balanchine's *The Nutcracker*, Le Clercq wore an abbreviated new tutu that was a sensational showcase for her legginess. It reminded audiences anew that the seemingly fixed forms of classical ballet costuming were constantly engaged in dialogue with contemporary women's clothes.

Classical ballet attire is distinct from most theatrical costume, comparable perhaps only to Kabuki in its ritualized separateness. Every classical tutu encompasses the most ceremonial and the most functional elements of dress and costume. The tutu holds in suspension a vestige of Baroque panniers and their projection of privileged indolence, as well as women's undergarments, heeding the need for the most functional and most economical covering. But since the ballet repertory is constantly expanding, even the classical tutu is subject to evolution, revision, experiment.

The Nutcracker premiered at the Mariinsky Theater in St. Petersburg in 1893, twenty years before Balanchine began studying at the company's allied academy. He danced in the Mariinsky production, but in 1954 he almost entirely rechoreographed it. For Le Clercq he created the role of Dewdrop to lead the women's ensemble in the "Waltz of the Flowers" divertissement in the second act. The novel costume that Karinska designed for her, as Karinska's biographer Toni Bentley writes, reflected the costumier's interest in women's corsets as well as her recent designs for Gypsy Rose Lee.[25] The bodice, featuring vertical boned seaming, sat atop a minimal skirt that was like a crunchy Elizabethan ruff. Its brevity startled fellow dancers and audiences alike.

In Balanchine's *La Valse*, Le Clercq's Girl in White was a singularly innocent and decadent anti-heroine who met her demise when Death visited a ballroom of whirling waltzers. Premiering in February 1951, it became one of her most

Tanaquil Le Clercq in the role of Dewdrop in New York City Ballet's production of *The Nutcracker*, 1954.

iconic roles and one of her favorites. Karinska's costume added to the spell that the ballet cast on the performers and the audience alike. Le Clercq and the entire women's ensemble wore long, bell-shaped ball gowns with multilayered tulle skirts. The ensemble's gowns were in multiple plummy shades misted with a pale overlay. Le Clercq's was oyster-colored, and over it she donned a black chiffon coat that was a courtship gift from Death. The bell-shaped tulle ball gowns suspended the dancers in an ambiguous time warp, simultaneously suggesting contemporary New Look evening gowns, voluminous historical precedents, and Romantic ballet costumes of the mid-nineteenth century. *La Valse* was a kinetic transposition of Gothic horror and febrile Romanticism containing a universal cautionary tale for humanity six years after the Axis surrender. Karinska's costumes allowed the ballet to generate the widest application and resonance (see page 86).

Le Clercq's identities as ballerina, photographer, model, wife, and muse are referenced in a photo taken by Balanchine soon after they married. She sits against the clapboard exterior of their modest, prefabricated country house set in beautiful acreage in Weston, Connecticut. We are literally seeing her through his eyes, but we are also watching them collaborate. Ballet is the most collaborative of art forms. In the rehearsal studio, Balanchine's dancers learned to enlarge,

amplify, and finish his choreographic sentences when they worked together on a new ballet. Le Clercq's photographic portraits of her husband were frequently published. Thus in this portrait, the roles of subject and object are reversed, even as husband and wife maintain the objectification of choreographer toward ballerina.

Le Clercq's expression seems utterly transparent—not assumed—enigmatic, perhaps somewhat wary, and ambiguous in the contact it makes with Balanchine's lens. She's wearing a print sundress and is as immaculately groomed as any fashion model, movie star—or ballerina. Yet at the same time her freckles show through. Her arms are formally composed but slightly restless, one shoulder strap is slipping from her shoulder, and her head is tilted askance. Façade and inner persona conjoin and merge.

Balanchine's medium close-up expands in the mind's eye to a panoramic vista: Le Clercq in context with her highly distinctive ballerina colleagues. With style and dash they brought the finest in American culture to the world's attention. Balanchine was boss, but they were the instruments that made his work possible. Their style onstage and off identified them as serious artists, creatures of allure and enchantment. They were independent personalities and personae. They were mutually dependent collaborators with their choreographers, their artistic director, and their storied, timeless, and topical art form.

George Balanchine's photograph of Tanaquil Le Clercq, ca. 1953.

AMERICAN BALLET AND READY-TO-WEAR FASHION, 1940S–1950S

PATRICIA MEARS

American ballet and fashion came into their own during World War II. And both flourished in the cultural capital of the United States, New York City. Thanks to the creative output of mid-century female fashion designers and the influence of ballerinas, a unique American design idiom arose that went on to impact culture and style for decades after the war and far beyond the borders of New York.

Ballet and fashion had different histories in America before the 1940s. Ballet was a burgeoning field that had just begun to take shape, whereas the American fashion industry was the world's largest; its production, distribution, promotion, and international buying power were unrivaled. Yet the American fashion machine did not have the cachet and artistry of Parisian haute couture, even though much of its output echoed French design. Then Paris, the undisputed capital of women's high fashion, was invaded by the Nazis, and American retailers, manufacturers, and fashion editors no longer had access to the latest couture innovations. There was no option but to support homegrown talent. Some of the best, such as Claire McCardell, Valentina, and Vera Maxwell, more than filled the void, producing work that clearly reflected the rise of dance in this country.

Although Americans did create fashions that were exclusive and made-to-order, most garments produced in the United States even before the war were not custom-made. Arguably, America's best and most innovative fashions were affordable, ready-to-wear designs that were marketed to the upper, middle, and working classes alike. This creative diversity was almost unheard of outside of the United States before the 1960s, and it is a testament to the nation's outstanding innovativeness and manufacturing might.

American ballet lagged behind fashion, but, thanks to the influx of exceptional émigrés who were able to train and promote homegrown talent, American classical dance quickly became globally recognized and influential. As in Great Britain, American ballet was built upon a Russian foundation, but its style was distinctly different from any other. Much credit for this goes to George Balanchine, co-founder and longtime director of New York City Ballet. Although many other ballet companies came into existence before and

after World War II—including NYCB's rival, Ballet Theatre (renamed American Ballet Theatre in 1957)—Balanchine did more than any other single individual to redirect and reshape the look of modern ballet in the United States and beyond.

Born in 1904, Mr. B, as he was affectionately called, was a product of the Imperial Russian system. He arrived in New York in 1934 and is widely considered to have been the greatest classical dance choreographer of the twentieth century. He implemented a new style of ballet, groomed a new kind of ballerina, and spearheaded a new style in ballet costumes. Sleek and speedy, his dancers and his choreography stripped away the decorative vestiges of Imperial style to reveal the essence of classical dance in a new, more articulated form.

Balanchine did not advance American ballet in a vacuum. He was among an elite group of Russian émigrés—dancers and teachers, musicians and composers, designers and artists—who did much to popularize ballet in the United States, just as they had in Western Europe. Ballet, like high fashion, had once seemed an art form unlikely to flourish in this country. A product of the great monarchies of Europe, it was as ostensibly elite and un-American as anything could be. Yet New York became a classical ballet capital, and dance schools and regional companies thrived around the country.

The groundwork for standalone ballet companies in America was laid half a century before Balanchine arrived in New York in the mid-1930s. The first notable company in the United States was the Metropolitan Opera Ballet, founded in 1883. It was created in the mold of the world's biggest opera companies, including the Paris Opera and La Scala in Milan, which have resident ballet troupes. However, these ballet companies operated differently from the Metropolitan Opera Ballet in that they not only performed in operas but also had independent, dance-only seasons of their own. Although the Metropolitan Opera Ballet was less like classical repertory companies such as New York City Ballet or American Ballet Theatre, it set the template for the presentation of full-length classical ballets, wielded considerable influence, and was an early leader in the production of classics such as *Les Sylphides*.

The Ballet Russe de Monte Carlo, one of the most important offshoots of Diaghilev's original Ballets Russes, was instrumental in bringing classical dance to hundreds of cities and small towns across North and South America during World War II. Stranded in the Western Hemisphere in 1940, the company performed numerous one-act works and truncated full-length ballets on stages ranging from the old Metropolitan Opera House in New York and the Hollywood Bowl in Los Angeles to high school gymnasiums in the middle of the country. American audiences were able to see for the first time true classical works performed by some of the era's greatest ballerinas, including Alexandra Danilova, Alicia Markova, and Irina Baronova.

Ballet became so popular in America that leading ballerinas appeared regularly in feature films and eventually on television from the 1920s to the 1960s. Many Hollywood movies included ballet and other dance sequences performed by Vera Zorina, Tamara Toumanova, Sono Osato, Melissa Hayden, and others. And leading actresses with little or no ballet training starred as ballerinas in an array of movies: Greta Garbo in *Grand Hotel* (1932) and Vivien Leigh in *Waterloo Bridge* (1940) are but two examples. Some former dancers successfully transitioned from dancer to actor, such as Audrey Hepburn, Brigitte Bardot, and especially Leslie Caron, who, like Cyd Charisse, performed ballet works in American movie musicals, which remained popular through the 1950s.

Perhaps the greatest testament to ballet's ascension and integration into American culture is the way *The Nutcracker* became synonymous with Christmas. The ballet was created by the same artists responsible for *The Sleeping Beauty* and the revised (and much improved) *Swan Lake*: choreographer Marius Petipa and composer Piotr Ilich Tchaikovsky. Despite its illustrious pedigree, the ballet had never been very popular in Russia. It was Americans who adopted and transformed it into the one of the most beloved and child-friendly ballets in history. The first production in the States was an abridged version by the Ballet Russe de Monte Carlo in 1940. A full-length version by Lew Christensen for the San Francisco Ballet debuted in 1944. But it was Balanchine's 1954 version that made *The Nutcracker* a national phenomenon. It was televised in 1958, with the choreographer starring as the benevolent gift giver, Herr Drosselmeyer. Though

he re-choreographed much of the ballet and simplified the storyline, Balanchine retained some of the most beautiful Imperial Russian elements, such as the "Waltz of the Snowflakes," which he remembered from his childhood.

Two elements that helped Balanchine's *Nutcracker* become the gold standard were the lavish sets and costumes. The latter were designed by the choreographer's long-time collaborator, Barbara Karinska. Together, they altered all forms of the ballerina's costume, eventually creating the New York City Ballet's signature skirt—the soft and malleable "powder-puff" tutu. Not only did it replace the rigid pancake tutu, constructed like a couture gown and favored by international ballet companies, but it also incorporated the more practical aspects of American fashion and its reliance on function and ready-to-wear innovation.

Although *The Nutcracker* is just one example of the full-length story ballets Balanchine created or revised, he is perhaps better known for his "leotard ballets." He did not originate leotards, but he did as much as anyone to popularize their use in ballet performances. A number of his masterpieces—*Concerto Barocco* (1941), *The Four Temperaments* (1946), *Agon* (1957), and *Square Dance* (1957)—were initially staged with lavish, at times cumbersome costumes. Only later were they performed in off-the-rack practice leotards and tights, sometimes with short practice skirts for the women. This paring down was not always a deliberate choice on Balanchine's part, but rather a practical solution when there was not enough money to commission tutus and other elaborate costumes. Leotards not only highlighted his ballerinas' lightning-fast footwork and extended leg line but also mirrored the activewear worn with increasing frequency throughout the country.

The parallels between informal ballet practice attire and American activewear during the 1940s are quite apparent. At the heart of the new aesthetic was a concept that typifies American fashion: function. Americans opted for adaptable clothing that could be readily purchased, slipped on with little fuss, and worn day-to-evening in most environmental conditions. At the same time, these fashions looked smart and fit well. In much the same way as mass production took hold in

the first half of the twentieth century, functionality became something of a national ideal, and most American fashion designers began to incorporate it into their creative mindset, designing clothing that met the needs of the entire multiethnic, increasingly mobile population throughout the vast and varied geography of the country.

The great industrialization of fashion in the United States was a multidimensional phenomenon. In addition to mass production, the birth and spread of coast-to-coast retailing meccas—Bergdorf Goodman and Saks Fifth Avenue in New York, Neiman Marcus in Texas, Marshall Field's in Chicago, and Bullock's in California—the booming field of advertising, which did much to promote "American" fashion and style, and even Hollywood films all contributed to the aura of American fashion and subsequent dissemination of a national style of dress.

The wide variety of fashion options available to consumers in the United States developed in part because of

NYCB principal dancers Allegra Kent and Arthur Mitchell in George Balanchine's *Agon*, 1972.

the changing social structure that American women were instrumental in creating. More and more women were being educated, playing sports, entering the workforce, and populating new domestic landscapes such as the suburbs. Their fashion needs and tastes helped to determine what came to be viewed as "American style."

In some ways, classical ballet in America mirrored the range and sophistication of its fashion industry. Though New York was the country's cultural capital, many other cities were important centers of fashion innovation and production. Rochester, Philadelphia, and Chicago were leaders in menswear manufacturing. Cities in the Northwest such as Seattle and Portland were home to sportswear and activewear firms that patented an array of cutting-edge designs. And California, especially Los Angeles, not only had a host of firms that created sportswear and custom-made clothing but also was home to the world's leading film industry and perhaps the most sophisticated movie costume ateliers. American fashion also reflected the changing aesthetics of its female clientele. Tall, lean, and leggy was the prevailing paradigm of both fashion and ballet.

By 1940, American fashions created by women were more available to the mainstream population than ever before. And no designer more clearly articulated the look of the modern, mobile American woman better than Claire McCardell. Slender and athletic, McCardell was also the physical embodiment of this new archetype; she wore the same easy, affordable, and highly functional sportswear that she designed for her clientele. Using deceptively simple construction techniques, McCardell not only pushed the aesthetic limits of what mass-produced clothing could look like but also helped to redefine the look of modern dressing.

McCardell was joined in the creation of cutting-edge sportswear by her contemporaries Mildred Orrick, Joset Walker, Vera Maxwell, Bonnie Cashin, and Tina Leser. All were accomplished working women who rejected the ideas espoused by the burgeoning cadre of Paris-based male couturiers, with their rigid formality and cumbersome ornamentation. These American women designers fully embraced the idea of comfortable daywear that middle- and even working-class people could afford. They mined non-Western costume and historical children's wear for sources that would help them design and manufacture handsome clothing that provided excellent fit without the expense and time required for custom-made fashion.

Although McCardell was a ready-to-wear designer, she understood and greatly appreciated the efforts of Parisian couturier Madeleine Vionnet, the brilliant technician who pioneered the art of draping and crafted the most innovative and kinetically advanced fashions during the interwar years. Vionnet's couture approach, however, entailed time-consuming workmanship that could not be economically replicated. McCardell came up with an array of solutions, many of which reflected ballet's influence, especially after she left the employ of Hattie Carnegie, one of the elite fashion retail houses that replicated Parisian couture designs even as it produced in-house originals.

In 1940 McCardell was rehired as the designer for Townley Frocks, a Seventh Avenue manufacturer that had closed in 1938, owing to an early McCardell success—the monastic dress (the garment was so successful that it fueled a multitude of cheaper knockoffs that drove Townley out of business). After she negotiated a new deal in which her name would appear on the label along with the manufacturer's, McCardell's work entered a new and distinctive phase. She crafted movement-friendly hoodies, capri pants, wrap dresses, travel-ready wardrobes, and even ballet slippers. Ballet also inspired one of her earliest design decisions, something that became a staple of her collections from then on: the use of knits.

For the duration of her career, McCardell produced tops, dresses, jumpers, leggings, and even swimwear using knitted woolens. Some of the earliest examples were featured on magazine covers geared toward teenagers and young women. One famous ensemble, created with a young college co-ed in mind, consisted of a full-length, ballet-inspired bodysuit of wool jersey, covered by a Tabard-style woven wool dress. Some fashion historians believe the bodysuit idea originally came from McCardell's close friend designer Mildred Orrick. Whoever was the originator, McCardell's version appeared both in *Harper's Bazaar* and on the cover of *Life* magazine in 1943.[1] Other designs more clearly illustrated a connection to

Pink rayon ready-to-wear evening dress by Tina Leser. Collection of Beverley Birks.

OPPOSITE: Nylon knitted bathing suit by Claire McCardell, 1948.
ABOVE: College co-eds wearing Claire McCardell knitted separates inspired by dancers' leotards and tights. *Harper's Bazaar*, August 1943.

dance class and rehearsal clothing. Fitted through the torso, waist, and hips, these one-piece garments were made with a variety of necklines, such as halters with open backs and deep V necks with no sleeves.

McCardell and Orrick were most likely aware of New York's vibrant dance culture, but to what extent? The British-born, Russian-trained ballerina Alicia Markova was noted for the knitted tops and leg warmers that she created and hand-crafted herself (her biographer asserts that she was the first person to design them). Markova was a well-known celebrity whose advice about makeup and self-styled appearance was featured in women's-interest magazines. And images of her in rehearsal wearing her handmade knitwear appeared in fashion magazines as early as 1938.[2]

McCardell's desire to eliminate the need for custom-fitted clothing went beyond knitwear. Working with woven fabrics that were considerably less flexible than knits, as well as with knitted woolens and synthetics, she employed a decades-old stratagem: the use of straps, from wide bands to spaghetti-width strings, that could be slung over the neck or circled around the waist and then tied, to provide the wearer with individualized fit and to adhere to the prevailing wasp-waisted silhouettes of the day. McCardell's strap-wrapped day dresses and evening gowns were also evocative of the Grecian-style dresses by Vionnet and fellow couturière Madame Grès.

No McCardell creation illustrated the impact of classical dance on fashion better than the "ballerina" slipper. This style of footwear, worn by millions today, was based on an actual dance shoe. Its creation was serendipitous. The United States, like virtually all countries engaged in World War II, imposed restrictions on materials such as silk, wool, and leather because they were essential to the military effort. Very few items of dress were exempt; one of them happened to be bal-let slippers. According to a number of sources, McCardell was unable to procure appropriate footwear for one of her early fashion presentations until she stumbled across the idea of using dance footwear by the New York–based firm Capezio.

The company was founded in 1887, when seventeen-year-old Italian émigré Salvatore Capezio opened a shoe repair shop specializing in theatrical footwear near the old

ABOVE: Copy of Claire McCardell's "Diaper" bathing suit in wool jersey, 1942. OPPOSITE: Wool bathing suit by Claire McCardell. *Harper's Bazaar*, May 1946.

opposite: Red and orange wool jersey swimsuit by Claire McCardell, ca. 1950. above: Bathing suit by Claire McCardell, 1950.

LEFT: Pleated-nylon
Empire-waist evening
dress by Claire
McCardell, ca. 1950.
OPPOSITE: Yellow and
gold rayon faille evening
dress and bolero by
Claire McCardell, 1949.

Metropolitan Opera House in New York City. Eventually he began constructing custom-made versions for professional dancers. By the 1930s, Capezio was producing shoes for Broadway musicals and the Ziegfeld Follies.

Capezio's move from the stage to the streets occurred in the early 1940s, and a number of sources credit Claire McCardell with this transition. In the introduction to McCardell's style guide, *What Shall I Wear?*, it states that, "in 1942 she started the craze for ballet slippers . . . because of wartime shortages to get the proper shoes for her show-room models."[3] Other sources credit legendary fashion editor Diana Vreeland with the idea of ballet shoes as streetwear and contend that Vreeland encouraged McCardell to adopt it during the war. Indeed, a full-page image of leather ballet slippers (along with an array of street shoes in a similar style) appeared in the July 1941 issue of *Harper's Bazaar*, where Vreeland was the editor in charge of American fashion. The caption read: "Ballet slippers—like Pavlova's, like the Degas ballerinas', like the black kid one on the opposite page—have inspired the most enchanting shoes. We have tied in our waist, our hair, our shoulders with ribbons [*sic*]. Now the time has come to tie up our ankles. The new ballet shoes may be worn at any time day or night."[4]

What is not in dispute was the success of this marriage of ballet and fashion. It was so successful, in fact, that McCardell was commissioned by Salvatore Capezio to design the slippers in fabrics that matched her garments. Major department stores such as Lord & Taylor and Neiman Marcus were selling other versions of Capezio footwear for women and, later, men. By 1949, Capezio shoes were featured on the cover of *Vogue*, and in 1952 Capezio received the Coty Award, the most prestigious honor in fashion at the time. Few original McCardell and Capezio examples survive in museum collections today, possibly owing to the shoes' popularity—women likely wore them out.[5] Ballet slippers have been a fashion staple ever since.

Another ballet-shoe manufacturer, Repetto, based in Paris, followed the Capezio template. The company's founder, Rose, mother of ballet dancer and choreographer Roland Petit, debuted her dance-shoe collection in 1947, the year that Dior presented his first New Look collection. In 1956 Repetto made the Cendrillon (Cinderella) shoe for Brigitte Bardot, a classically trained dancer, who wore them in her breakout film, *Et Dieu . . . créa la femme*. The company continued to produce shoes for celebrities, entered into collaborations with designers such as Issey Miyake and Rei Kawakubo, and remains one of the leading makers of ballerina slippers today.

Other American designers who looked to ballet dancers as sources of inspiration were themselves dancers before turning to fashion. One was Vera Maxwell. The daughter of Austrian immigrants, Vera Huppe was born in 1901 and began her ballet training in New York City. In 1919 she became a member of the Metropolitan Opera Ballet, remaining with the company until her marriage to financier Raymond J. Maxwell in 1924. Before her early retirement from the stage, Maxwell starting modeling for the department store B. Altman. She observed that when "the opera season ended in May, the fashion houses on Seventh Avenue were just opening their collections. I would just walk across the street and hire on as a model."[6] Around 1929, Maxwell began sketching for the fashion houses she had modeled for and eventually took up design, working anonymously for clothing manufacturers before opening her eponymous line in 1947; she retired four decades later.

During her heyday in the 1950s and 1960s, Maxwell's work echoed that of contemporaries McCardell, Clare Potter, Mildred Orrick, Joset Walker, Tina Leser, Carolyn Schnurer, and Bonnie Cashin, all masters of functional sportswear. And although much of Maxwell's output was geared toward sports, travel, and the modern urban lifestyle, it also reflected ballerinas' practice clothing. Leotards, leggings, and wrapped tops were the inspiration for ensembles such as the gray knitted pieces in the collection of The Museum at FIT. And more formal garments such as a dress with a jersey top and full, floor-length skirt look like dressy versions of ballet practice clothes.

Another American couturier who incorporated balletic elements into her creations was Valentina Schlee. Born Valentina Nicholaevna Sanina (purportedly in 1899) in Kiev, she was known professionally by her first name. After fleeing the 1917 Revolution, Valentina made her way to the United States in 1923 and began her fashion and theatrical design career in 1928. Throughout the 1930s and until she closed her

"The Ballet Slipper," *Harper's Bazaar*, July 1941.

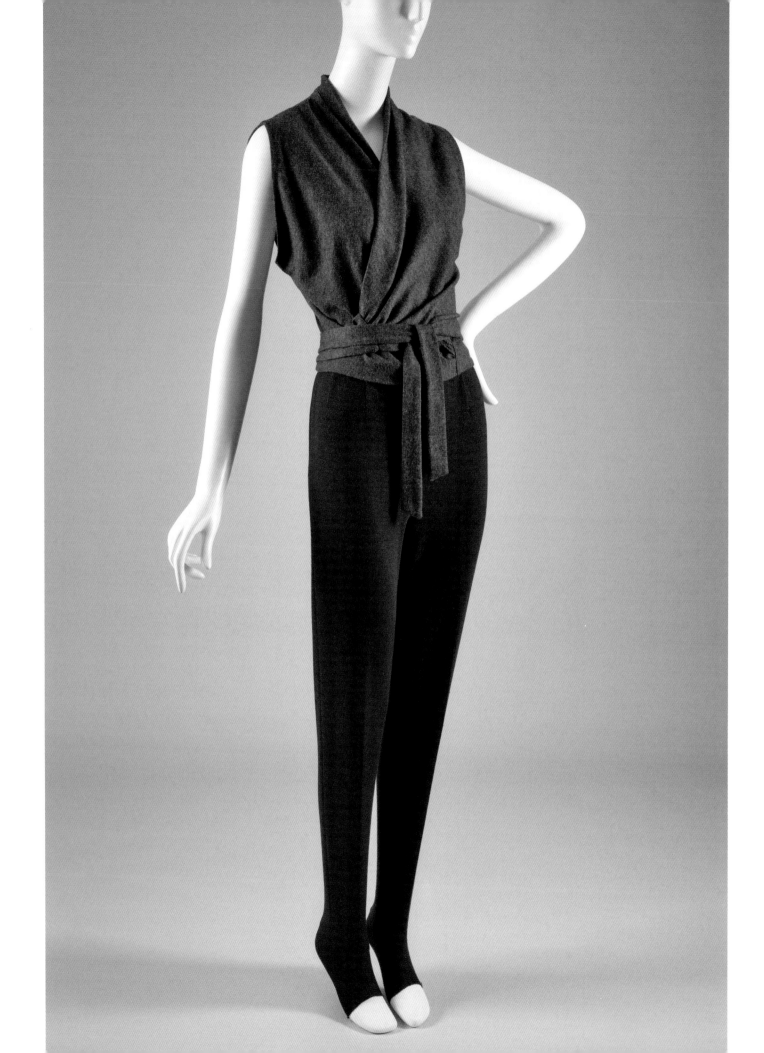

OPPOSITE: Wool knit top and pants ensemble by Vera Maxwell, ca. 1955.
ABOVE: Wool jersey and silk satin evening dress by Vera Maxwell, designed for her Speed Suit label, 1975.

Valentina and Garbo rather closely resembled each other and lived in the same New York City apartment building.

In terms of fashion, Valentina was one of the most distinctively stylish women in New York—and one of the most categorical, prone to such memorable pronouncements as: "Yellow is for flowers," "Children are for suburbs," and "Mink is for football." Her designs were noted for their austere simplicity and their ease when worn, as well as for their minimalist and sculptural qualities. When the designer wore examples of her own somewhat outrageous headwear, like wimples and coolie hats, her work appeared even more dramatic, with a decidedly monastic air.

Valentina's seamless blend of function and drama may have stemmed from her early connections to the theater. A number of sources note that she studied ballet and acting before embarking on a short-lived theatrical career in tsarist Russia. After fleeing to Western Europe, then America, she not only created clothes but also wore and modeled them to great effect. Her declaration "I am theater" was a shout that emanated from nearly all her designs. And ballet was deeply embedded in her work. Curator Phyllis Magidson wrote: "Valentina mined the conceits of nineteenth-century theatrical costuming, reintroducing to contemporary fashion such role-defining period elements as the cross-lacing 'peasant' girdle (Giselle, La Sylphide, and Coppelia); ballet-length skirts (Swan Lake, Les Sylphides); medieval high-waisted, corsage baring [sic] bodices; and cascading bell and balloon sleeves (Romeo and Juliet, Othello.)"[7]

American mid-century fashion designers produced many examples of clothing, high and low, inspired by ballet attire. Women creators based in New York were the leaders in adapting balletic elements, whereas in Paris and London, both male and female couturiers incorporated features of ballet costume into their work. A new generation of American women designers continued to make ballet-style clothing from the 1960s to the 1980s, modifying it to meet the ever-changing needs of modern women.

house in the late 1950s, Valentina was one of the most exclusive dressmakers in New York. She was also a mysterious figure, whose marriage to Russian financier George Schlee might be the best-known part of her legacy, as he reputedly had a long-term affair with Greta Garbo. Interestingly,

ABOVE: Black rayon dress by Valentina Schlee. *Harper's Bazaar*, March 1944. OPPOSITE: Detail of a black jersey dress by Valentina Schlee, ca. 1944.

WAIFS AND MODS: BALLET AND FASHION, 1960s–1970s

PATRICIA MEARS

The 1960s and 1970s were decades of momentous change. Both fashion and ballet were directly affected by the era's seismic political, social, demographic, and cultural shifts. Every aspect of the American and European clothing industries was profoundly altered as fashion became more accessible and youth oriented, but also more financially driven. Classical ballet in the West underwent important changes but remained popular and influential. This was especially true in New York, where the 1970s was a golden age for all dance forms, from disco to Broadway to classical ballet. In many ways, ballet and fashion navigated the changing times together.

Early in the 1960s, the New York–based fashion industry began a concerted effort to promote its leading designers. This bold move was an attempt to adopt France's time-honored practice of celebrating its artistic creators while simultaneously reducing the power of American clothing manufacturers who tended to conceal their designers from the public. A primary catalyst for this change was the founding of the Council of Fashion Designers of America (CFDA) in 1962. Spearheaded by pioneering fashion publicist Eleanor Lambert, and with a membership of just over fifty of America's leading fashion design talents, the CFDA's primary mandate was the recognition and promotion of fashion designers based in the United States. Its high-profile membership and newsworthy activities paralleled the ascendancy of American fashion's global influence, which occurred during one of the richest cultural periods in United States history.

Lambert used American fashion's link to classical ballet—and high culture in general—to advance the CFDA. In 1964, acting on an idea proposed by President John F. Kennedy before his death, Senators Jacob Javits and Claiborne Pell helped establish the National Council on the Arts (NCA). Lambert attended one of the first meetings of the new Special Subcommittee on the Arts, during which choreographer "Maggie [Agnes] de Mille, represented dance and was brilliant," Lambert recalled. "I've never heard such an eloquent speech about one artist by another. She wanted the council to pay for a sabbatical for Jerome Robbins, which was approved, and it was during that time that he choreographed the ballets *Dances at a Gathering* and the *Schoenberg Variations* [*sic*]."[1] Lambert believed that fashion was a creative entity as deserving of recognition by the NCA as painting, music, and dance. She knew, however, that only not-for-profit (i.e., artistic) organizations were eligible for NCA consideration. Commercial industries were not.

The CFDA fulfilled the "artistic" requirement by hosting collaborative fashion and performing-arts events. One such event, in honor of American Ballet Theatre, took place on Sunday, September 25, 1966. Titled *Fashion and Broadway Salute the ABT*, the show was staged at the St. James Theater and hosted by Lauren Bacall. Ballets, including George Balanchine's *Theme and Variations*, Jerome Robbins's *Fancy Free*, and Agnes de Mille's "Skating Scene" from *The Wind in the Mountains*, alternated with fashion shows such as *All Black* and *The High Pastels* that highlighted works by CFDA members. Senator Javits and other attendees enthusiastically praised the event for its professional quality and the beauty of both the dance and the fashion components.

One reason the evening was so successful was that former first lady Jacqueline Kennedy was the event's honorary chair. Lambert understood the power of celebrity, and Mrs. Kennedy was one of the most recognized and admired women in the world. But the subtler power of Kennedy's participation lay in her reputation as a champion of the arts and high culture. She and President Kennedy had helped to promulgate the importance of the arts in America and accelerate their acceptance. The promotion of fashion was part of this cultural upsurge, and Lambert, who had strong connections to the art world since her early days as a publicist, as well as an uncanny ability to read the zeitgeist, took full advantage.

While American fashion was shifting into a designer-driven industry in the 1960s, the rise of youth culture and the upending of rigid social norms led to a major restructuring of the clothing industry in Europe. Ready-to-wear fashion became widely available to consumers for the first time, and the proliferation of small, designer-owned boutiques in London emerged as a newsworthy trend. British ballet was quick to reflect this new cultural and business climate.

VOGUE

YOUNG IDEAS

CONTEST: VOGUE LOOKS FOR MODELS

APRIL 1959 · PRICE 3/6

THE CONDÉ NAST PUBLICATIONS LTD.

The vibrant cover of the April 1959 issue of British *Vogue* heralded the changing mood. Two young Royal Ballet soloists, Georgina Parkinson and Hylda Zinkin, mirroring each other as they leap in the air with jubilantly arched backs, wear colorful, male-inspired leisure clothing. Both the photo and its caption ("It's a huge jump of joy for our special Young Ideas issue") exemplify the vigor and casualness of the coming British Youthquake movement, which would eclipse the glamour and formality of 1950s couture.

Around the same time, the Royal Ballet in London lost its visionary and imperious leader, Ninette de Valois, who retired in 1963. Frederick Ashton assumed the directorship, a position he held until his abrupt dismissal in 1970. The great classical repertory for which he became world famous was expanded during this period. In 1960 he choreographed a modernized version of the oldest continuously performed ballet, *La Fille mal gardée* (or The Wayward, or Unchaperoned, Daughter), originally choreographed by Jean Dauberval in 1789. A charming piece, it starred the young and technically precocious South African–born ballerina Nadia Nerina.

In 1965 Ashton created one of his greatest modernist masterpieces, *Monotones*. Set to the music of Erik Satie, the ballet's pas de trois for two men and one woman was a hit, in part because of the costumes: white, full-body leotards and helmets covered with large gems. Influenced by space exploration and Balanchine's ultramodern "leotard" ballets, Ashton understood that fashions had changed dramatically since his heyday, the 1930s to the 1950s. London was now leading the unisex trend: long hair for men and androgynous clothing for both genders. Ashton caught and rode the unisex wave in his choreography. He added a second pas de trois (this time for two women and one man), and both trios moved with a slowness that evoked recent film imagery of astronauts walking in outer space. Although men had not yet walked on the moon, *Monotones* anticipated the event so well that within a few years Ashton erroneously "told an interviewer that his choreography was influenced by the time 'when you Americans were all landing on the moon.'"[2]

It was also during the 1960s that Margot Fonteyn entered the last, unexpectedly successful, phase of her career. The ballerina had turned forty at the end of the 1950s and was seriously contemplating retirement, in part because her long collaboration with Frederick Ashton was beginning to falter. His ballet *Ondine* (1958), choreographed for her, was not well received, even though the ballerina was lauded for her lyrical performance as the water sprite for which the work was named (see page 26).

As Ashton was marginalizing Fonteyn, one of the most noteworthy events in modern ballet history occurred: in 1961 star Soviet dancer Rudolph Nureyev defected to the West. De Valois, still the guiding force of the Royal Ballet, decided that Fonteyn and Nureyev would become dance partners. Controversial at the time, many, including Fonteyn herself, did not believe it was a prudent decision. The two dancers were vastly different in age (she was forty-two; he, twenty-four), training (he was a product of the Kirov, as the Mariinsky was known in the Soviet era, the venerated institution that had produced the greatest ballets and dancers of the preceding century, while she was a formative member of the relatively new British school), and temperament (Fonteyn had a "tea-with-the-queen" air,[3] whereas Nureyev was fierce and fiery). But yet again, de Valois's vision was inspired and prescient, resulting in the greatest partnership in modern classical ballet. Not only did Fonteyn and Nureyev reinvigorate the classics, but they also became box-office gold. Indeed, Nureyev's rendition of the male roles in traditional ballets generated such excitement that the phenomenon was nicknamed "Princes' Lib." Balletomanes and new converts to ballet alike camped out each time they performed, eager to secure tickets, just like the burgeoning wave of rock 'n' roll fans.

As ballet was changing, so, too, was the fashion aesthetic of leading ballerinas. As noted in Rosemary Harden's essay, Fonteyn remained a couture client; after the death of Christian Dior in 1957, she turned to Yves Saint Laurent. A wunderkind who took over the house of Dior in 1958 before opening his own house in 1962, Saint Laurent would become a dominant force in fashion for the next two decades. Fonteyn embraced his avant-garde and sometimes racy fashion novelties just as her sexy, electric partnership with Nureyev was taking off.

Royal Ballet prima ballerina Margot Fonteyn's wool jersey "Mondrian" dress by Yves Saint Laurent, 1965.

Though Fonteyn never completely shed her elegant and restrained style, the 1960s was a liberating period for the middle-aged dancer, both professionally and sartorially. In 1965 she was named to the world's best-dressed list, wearing "good" coats and practical knitwear by Saint Laurent, as well as garments from his newsworthy Mondrian collection and provocative eveningwear. An example of the latter was a sheer organza cocktail dress ornamented with strategically placed, zigzag bands of embroidered sequins. Even when Fonteyn and Nureyev were arrested in San Francisco (the two were attending a party in the Haight-Ashbury neighborhood and were caught up in a drug bust by the police), she was wearing a Saint Laurent ensemble. Such off-duty antics did little if anything to tarnish their image. Overall, publicity was instrumental in maintaining the ballet's status and popularity, as postwar aesthetics and tastes were undergoing dramatic change. Youthquake influences were overtaking historically inspired couture, and both Fonteyn and Nureyev dressed the part.

The expansion of balletomania was also propelled by Soviet dancers who began performing in the West in the 1950s. Two especially influential stars were Galina Ulanova and Maya Plisetskaya, who was the first Soviet ballerina to don Parisian couture. As noted in the Introduction, Soviet-era ballerinas had had little collective impact on high fashion. The production of high-end goods like fashion, accessories, and jewelry all but ceased after the 1917 Revolution. And Soviet dancers had little exposure to Western fashion, even after they began to tour Western Europe and the Americas.

As the Cold War brinkmanship between the Soviet Union and the United States revved up, cultural exchanges also increased, including tours by leading companies and individual dancers performing as guest artists. For example, Beryl Grey, a principal with the Royal Ballet, toured the Soviet Union in 1957, the first British dancer to do so. In addition to performances with regional companies, she danced the role of Odette/Odile in *Swan Lake* with the Bolshoi Ballet in Moscow and the Kirov Ballet in Leningrad.

One of the most heralded tours was the Bolshoi Ballet's in 1956. After engagements in Asia and Eastern Europe, the company performed in London to sold-out audiences. The Bolshoi's prima ballerina was Galina Ulanova, who won over British fans with her astonishingly beautiful dancing in productions such as *Romeo and Juliet.* So convincing was her performance as a teenage girl (although she was in her mid-forties at the time) that Margot Fonteyn rushed backstage to congratulate her. The startled Ulanova was unaware that the effusive fan was her British equivalent. The daughter of a ballerina born and raised under the tsarist regime, Ulanova became the queen of Soviet culture. Yet her appearance off-stage was plain and mousy, so it is not surprising that despite her greatness, Ulanova had no impact on the fashion world.

This was decidedly not true of her younger compatriot Maya Plisetskaya. Unlike Ulanova, who was trained in the purer, more classically refined Mariinsky style, Plisetskaya was a Bolshoi dancer through and through. Bold and vivacious, she embodied the company's dynamic, athletic, and highly expressive style. And her looks were as dramatic as her dancing.

Plisetskaya's road to ballet (and fashion) stardom was almost as dramatic as the ballets she starred in. Born in 1925, she had a horrific childhood. Her father was Mikhail Plisetsky, a Soviet official of Jewish descent, who was arrested in 1937 and executed the following year during the Great Purge. Her mother, actress Rachel Messerer, was arrested in 1938 and spent a few years in prison before being shipped to a labor camp with her infant son. Maya and her brother Alexander were destined for an orphanage until her aunt Sulamith Messerer took her in, and her uncle Asaf Messerer took in Alexander. Both aunt and uncle were principal dancers at the Bolshoi.

Plisetskaya was trained at the Bolshoi, joined the company at age eighteen, then quickly moved up the ranks, becoming the company's leading ballerina shortly after Ulanova's retirement in 1960. She was not, however, allowed to travel abroad with the company on their initial tours to Western Europe. Given her talent and family history, Soviet leader Nikita Khrushchev was initially fearful that she might defect. Plisetskaya convinced him of her patriotism, and the travel ban was lifted in 1959 on Khrushchev's personal intercession. To New York audiences, her dancing was a revelation.

Royal Ballet prima ballerina Margot Fonteyn's sequined silk gauze mini-dress by Yves Saint Laurent, 1966.

Khrushchev was immensely satisfied with the reviews of her performances. "He embraced her upon her return: 'Good girl, coming back. Not making me look like a fool. You didn't let me down.'"[4]

During her first visit to New York, the ballerina was featured in the September 1959 issue of *Harper's Bazaar*. This debut appearance was a full-length portrait by Richard Avedon. In it she appears to be nude, wrapped in a "czar's ransom of Russian lynx: a coat designed by Emeric Partos of Bergdorf Goodman."[5] The image is accompanied by an excerpt from the book *Observation*, featuring Avedon's photographs and Truman Capote's text. The writer noted that the ballerina had been not only kept from Western audiences but also sequestered in Moscow because of "an affair of the heart that hurled itself into scandal." Capote went on to write that she was reinstated due to the dedication and ardor of her fans, as well as "those who resented Plisetskaya's unsoviet and womanly glamour. . . this glittering animal, with her brilliantly abandoned control. . . brings out such an attractive audience, youthful and knowledgeable and excitingly demonstrative."[6] Capote captured the sentiments of Soviet and American dance fans, as well as fashion specialists.

Plisetskaya not only went on to appear regularly in Western fashion magazines throughout the 1960s but also developed relationships with the couturiers Pierre Cardin and Yves Saint Laurent. The impact of the Russian ballerina on Saint Laurent's work is perhaps not surprising. In Trapeze, his first collection as head designer of the house of Dior, the signature triangular or trapeze silhouette reflected the traditional Russian overdress, or *sarafan*, and a few of the garments were given Russian names such as "Nadezhda" and "Tatyana."

The following year, 1959, Saint Laurent became the first Western designer to bring his collection to the Soviet Union. Although only select members of society were permitted entrée to the private runway show, the general public had the opportunity to see the models when the collection was presented in Red Square and at the leading Soviet department store, GUM. As color images of the events illustrate, and as an online translation from a period source, *Ogoniok*, one of the main magazines of the time, reveals, the crowd appeared puzzled and a bit apprehensive:

> The audience watches the models with great attention: Some imagine trying on the dresses and slipping on the shoulders fur mantles, others try to remember an attractive pattern. The spectators note: "Why are the fur dresses so low-necked? That's nearly a sundress. For northerners like us that isn't really practical. And in summer it'll be too hot in such a dress, even in the evening. The dresses are a little bit too short. That won't be beautiful on short or plump women. The hand-made embroidery on tulle is without doubt very beautiful, but who can afford such an expensive dress?"[7]

Saint Laurent's most famous ode to Russian culture was his autumn/winter 1976 haute couture collection. Dedicated to Russian literary heroines such as Tolstoy's Natasha Rostova and Anna Karenina, as well as to Diaghilev's Ballets Russes, the rich, colorful, and opulent collection was more evocative of Cossack uniforms and traditional Russian peasant costumes than the exotic and modernist costumes of Léon Bakst, the early Ballets Russes artist and designer. Saint Laurent also dabbled in designing ballet costumes for Plisetskaya and the French ballerina Zizi Jeanmaire.

But Plisetskaya's relationship with Saint Laurent was not as profound as the collaboration and friendship that developed between her and Pierre Cardin. Best known for his Space Age looks and many licensing agreements, Cardin was an ardent ballet fan who reportedly traveled to Moscow some thirty times to see Plisetskaya perform at the Bolshoi Theater. Like Saint Laurent, Cardin designed couture and both ballet and film costumes, including those for a ballet production of *Anna Karenina*, for which he was not credited. Although their relationship is sparsely documented in the couturier's numerous exhibition catalogues and monographs, his designs for the ballerina were well publicized at the time. It is perhaps telling that Plisetskaya devoted an entire chapter of her autobiography to their working relationship. So little about their collaboration is actually known that one can only spec-

Bolshoi Ballet prima ballerina Maya Plisetskaya, New York, November 26, 1962. Photograph by Richard Avedon.

ulate whether she inspired creations such as the ivory feather capelet in The Museum at FIT's permanent collection. But it is likely that the couturier saw Plisetskaya dance two of her greatest roles—*The Dying Swan* solo and Odette/Odile in *Swan Lake*—attired in feather-trimmed tutus.

Plisetskaya's connection to Western fashion was just a blip on the radar. What the Soviet Union gave the world was the ballerina herself, both artistically and aesthetically. Few Soviet ballerinas may have worn couture, but they were as physically beautiful as any living beyond the Iron Curtain. Joel Lobenthal documents the physique of leading mid-century Soviet ballerinas in his biography of the Kirov star Alla Osipenko. Not only did she have what was deemed the world's most beautiful écarté (a straightened leg and pointed foot that extends to the side while the body is turned at a 45-degree angle from the viewer), but her body, like that of her compatriots, was beautifully proportioned overall.

In the 1960s, two of Balanchine's ballerinas—Allegra Kent and Mimi Paul—were exquisitely lyrical dancers who were regularly featured in *Vogue* and *Harper's Bazaar*. Trained and molded by Balanchine, they were the latest in a long line of inspirational muses. Beginning with Lydia Ivanova in the 1920s, Balanchine became fixated on a succession of dancers, including Vera Zorina, his third wife, in the 1930s, and Diana Adams and Tanaquil Le Clercq after World War II. Both Zorina and Le Clercq were favored by the fashion press and regularly appeared in top magazines.

Allegra Kent was one of Balanchine's 1960s favorites. Fleet-footed and flexible, she was asked by the choreographer to join the fledgling New York City Ballet at the tender age of fifteen. Two years later, in 1954, Balanchine choreographed the first major role for her to Charles Ives's *The Unanswered Question* in the ballet *Ivesiana*. Dressed only in a leotard with no shoes or accessories, Kent not only was praised for her dancing but also impressed the artist Joseph Cornell, who created a number of his renowned boxes inspired by her. The next work Balanchine choreographed for her made her a star: *The Seven Deadly Sins*. It debuted in 1958 and was "one of the theatrical events of the season." Soon afterward, Kent wrote in her autobiography, *Once a Dancer*, "Richard Avedon

wanted me to model for him, and eventually I would appear on four pages in *Harper's Bazaar* in fashionable outfits. . . . Kenneth the hairdresser did my hair in a jungle style, transforming me into Tarzan's Jane doing Pilates." She became ballet's gamine, crafting "an improvisational dance for the camera—a dance of self and sepia seersucker."[8] Her porcelain features resembled those of the era's top waif-like model, Ingrid Boulting (a Royal Ballet–trained dancer), despite what Kent described as botched facial surgery that her mother had forced upon her. And her personal style, such as her penchant for thrift-store finds that she self-styled with safety and clothes pins, was years ahead of other trendsetters.

The magic Kent projected on stage and in print belied her highly dysfunctional upbringing, torturous marriage to fashion photographer Bert Stern, and sometimes debilitating physical and mental health problems. The ballerina documented her tumultuous life in her surprisingly candid and reflective autobiography. Born Iris Cohen in 1937, she was of Polish Jewish descent but was raised as a Christian Scientist (her mother had converted) and regularly crisscrossed the American South with one or both of her parents until she moved to New York to begin training at NYCB's School of American Ballet. Kent married Stern when she was in her early twenties. She danced through his mental illness and drug addiction and the birth of their three children, but often sporadically.

Despite her crisis-filled life, Balanchine understood her special gifts and created other works for her such as *Bugaku*, the raciest and sexiest ballet of its time. Kent wrote that the ballet may have been based on images of her shot by Stern for a 1961 *Vogue* editorial spread. (He told Kent he was hired because of his marriage to her.[9]) In the photos, she sports an array of bouffant hairstyles and in one image wears a semisheer nightgown. Based on a ritual Japanese dance, *Bugaku* contains a "segment that represents a seduction and what might follow once the nightgown is removed." Karinska's costumes for the ballet were unlike anything else at the time. Under lacquered wigs, chrysanthemum-shaped tutus, and gauzy kimono-style robes, Kent wore a sheer bodysuit overlaid with a daisy-covered bikini. An image of the latter

Off-white ostrich feather and satin bolero by Pierre Cardin, ca. 1960.

OPPOSITE: NYCB principal dancers Allegra Kent and Edward Villella in George Balanchine's *Bugaku. Vogue,* August 15, 1963.
ABOVE: Allegra Kent in a nightgown. *Vogue, November 15, 1961.*

appeared in *Vogue* in 1963. The floral motifs were similar to those appliquéd onto kicky dresses and rompers by Saint Laurent and couturier Emanuel Ungaro in the 1960s. Stern's photos and Balanchine's ballet were produced when both men were "at the top of their form, and creative assignments came floating" Kent's way.[10]

If Kent had the wistful, ethereal look popular in the late 1960s, Mimi Paul was the American incarnation of the British "dolly girl," the era's other fashion archetype. Nearly 5 feet 7 inches tall and slender, with long feet, a mane of dark hair, and enormous doe-like eyes, Paul looked like a model. Indeed, she was featured in fashion magazines wearing costumes and couture with equal aplomb. Interestingly, Paul was Kent's alternate in *Bugaku* and was photographed in the role by Cecil Beaton for a 1966 issue of *Vogue*, one of a number of photographs he took of her featuring her long, swan-like neck. Paul may have made her fashion debut in the same November 1961 issue that featured Kent. Along with three other NYCB corps de ballet members, Paul modeled nightgowns while on pointe in the pages immediately following the Kent layout.

Paul may not be as well remembered as her contemporaries Allegra Kent and, especially, Suzanne Farrell, but she was nonetheless a brilliant dancer who was lauded by critics and balletomanes alike. The only child of Norman Paul, a Russian-born, French- and Swiss-educated physician, and Marguerite Pahud Paul, the owner of a fashion boutique in Washington, D.C., Mimi was a precocious talent who rose through the ranks, becoming a principal dancer with the New York City Ballet. And although she did not stay at NYCB for the duration of her career (she moved to American Ballet Theatre in 1969), Balanchine did choreograph memorable pieces for her, such as the beautifully lyrical variation in the "Emeralds" section of his full-length ballet *Jewels*. Existing photographs and rare moving images of her illustrate both her pristinely articulated lines and crisply fluid footwork.

Few American ballerinas were as frequently and prominently featured in fashion publications as Paul. The ballet and fashion fusion is less readily evident in an image of her by Gjon Mili, an Albanian immigrant known for his stroboscopic portraits of dancers in motion dating to the 1940s. This 1967 photograph was taken in the lobby of the New York State Theater (now the Koch Theater) at Lincoln Center, home of the New York City Ballet. Standing in front of one of the two monumental Elie Nadelman marble sculptures that dominate the lobby, Paul models a polka-dotted, silk chiffon evening dress by the Parisian couturière Madame Grès. The garment and the image are undeniably high fashion, but a subtle connection to ballet can be seen in the swirl of fabric Paul sweeps over her shoulder, illustrating the dancer within as well as the kinetic nature of Grès's work. The couturière, as it happens, had been interested in pursuing a dance career when she was young. She pioneered the softer and more fluid looks that infiltrated fashion throughout the 1960s.

The image of Paul that most effectively synthesized the ballerina and the mod fashion archetype is a Richard Avedon portrait of her. Featured in the April 15, 1969, issue of *Vogue*, she wears a black wool jumpsuit by Michael Mott for Paraphernalia (see page 196). Her torso is turned away from the camera so that the deeply scooped back of the garment shows off her lithe, slender ballet body to great advantage. The caption notes that the fashion looked "divine on a girl like Mimi Paul, with skin like camellias and the long pure line of neck and spine that could only belong to a ballerina. A principal dancer with the American Ballet Theater, she has, said Richard Avedon, who photographed her here, 'style, power, amusement. She is a great American beauty.'" Not just Paul's body and personality made her an ideal fashion model, but so did her pretty face, especially her expressive eyes. When her eyes were made up with extra-long lashes and rimmed with pronounced liner, her face resembled that of other leading models, such as Penelope Tree and Peggy Moffitt.

Paul believed that one reason she was featured so prominently in *Vogue* and *Harper's Bazaar* was her personal connection to Richard Avedon: she was married to his first cousin once removed, Michael Avedon, who was also a photographer. Kent agreed that their proximity to important fashion photographers played a role in their exposure. This notion, however, does not take into account the fact that they were celebrated artists who garnered fans and press years before their respective marriages or that their unique styles,

NYCB ballerina Allegra Kent in a dress by Leo Narducci. *Vogue*, April 15, 1970.

OPPOSITE: Silk
chiffon polka-dotted
evening dress by
Madame Grès, 1967.
RIGHT: NYCB ballerina
Mimi Paul wearing
Madame Grès's silk
chiffon evening
dress, New York State
Theater, 1967.

facial beauty, and magical abilities in front of the camera were not universal qualities.

As the mod sixties gave way to the louche seventies, fashion was set against the era's dour economic mood. This dichotomic decade—sandwiched between the counterculture 1960s and the opulent 1980s—witnessed the demise of haute couture's majestic reign and the ascension of designer-led conglomerates. The "shifting sands" of style in the 1970s accelerated the relaxation of fashion codes, as young people increasingly sought individuality by wearing an eclectic mélange of vintage clothing (now a stylistic mainstay) for the first time. Many women's wardrobes contained a pastiche of elements, including menswear, ethnic clothing, and historical revivals of the not-so-distant past, such as the streamlined styles of the interwar years. More than anything, fashions of the 1970s were blatantly sexy. The sexual revolution was reflected in an array of items that remain hallmarks of the era: halter necklines, tube tops, see-through blouses, hot pants, camisoles, knee-high boots, and the ballet leotard.

The one-piece torso covering that had long been the staple garment of dancers' practice clothes and of many modern ballets, the leotard became fashion's latest staple. An article that appeared in the June 18, 1979, issue of *People* magazine summed it up: "Candice Bergen wears her leotards to exercise class. Cheryl Tiegs modeled hers for the cover of TIME. Natalia Makarova practices at the barre in hers. Cher and Suzanne Somers like to shop Beverly Hills in theirs. Nowadays, the old-fashioned dance costume . . . is no longer basic black and one design. At Danskin, the nation's leading body-wear firm, the leotard has exploded with 10 fabrics, 78 colors, and 124 styles to become the uniform of the day (and night) for energized discoers, gymnasts, joggers, roller skaters and sedentary executives across the country."[11]

Read by millions, *People* was a publication that focused on pop culture and celebrities. Though the article featured a list of well-known women, including actresses, a singer, a model, and a ballerina, its focus was on "a green-eyed, red-haired, 31-year-old designer named Bonnie August,"[12] as the article's title, "Danskin Designer Bonnie August Has Got Almost Everybody Going Around in Next to Nothing," indicates.

The leotard may have been modernized during the 1970s, but it has been around for more than two hundred years. As popular as it became, relatively little has been written on the creation and evolution of this streamlined, knitted garment designed for ease of movement and modesty. The genesis of the leotard and tights dates back to the turn of the nineteenth century. Inspired by medieval leggings and costumes worn by circus performers, the head of the Paris Opera costume department, a Monsieur Maillot (his first name is unknown), crafted pale, "flesh"-colored knitted leggings and underwear that clung to the human form. The purpose of these underpinnings was to cover the naked body as the trend for featherweight neoclassical muslin gowns was replacing the corsets and panniered skirts of the ancien régime. Later, *maillot* became the French word for swimsuit.

The word *leotard* derives from the name of the pioneering French aerialist Jules Léotard. Born in 1838, in Toulouse, he abandoned a career in law to become an acrobatic performer and is credited with inventing the flying trapeze act. At the age of twenty-one, Léotard made his debut at the Cirque Napoléon[13] and went on to perform throughout Europe to great acclaim. His most lasting legacies, however, were a song written by George Leybourne in 1867 titled "The Daring Young Man on the Flying Trapeze" and the knitted, body-fitting, one-piece garment that today bears his name. The leotard did not become a ballet staple until the twentieth century, when the torso-covering garment was paired with wool or silk knitted leggings, or tights.

Though leotards were initially reserved for class or rehearsal, tights were worn onstage with tutus, as they provided a modicum of decency. According to Akim Volynsky, a Russian critic active during the late Imperial and early Bolshevik periods, tights did far more than cover the body's private parts. He wrote: "The ballerina's costume constitutes something extraordinary. The tights, which fit close to the legs, strike the spectator first and foremost, then the ballerina's flimsy dress, and finally, the pink ballet slippers without heels."[14]

Volynsky believed that when "clothed in tights . . . the smoothed out leg assembles itself into a compact, artistically working unit." More bluntly, he stated that "roughness

Portrait of NYCB ballerina Mimi Paul, ca. 1968.

Highly decorated costumes, both traditional and avant-garde, were still prevalent when Volynsky was writing during the 1920s, but the practice of wearing only leotards and tights for both rehearsal and performance was on the rise. In the post–World War II era, George Balanchine's leotard ballets became a staple of classical dance. The reliance on knitted costumes was beginning to grow just as knits were becoming more prevalent in women's high fashion and greater exposure of the body was becoming common. Perhaps the earliest ballet to set this trend was *Le Chant du Rossignol*, or *Song of the Nightingale*. Choreographed in 1925 by George Balanchine, it starred Diaghilev's handpicked baby ballerina, fourteen-year-old Alicia Markova. Her prepubescent body was clad in a diamante-trimmed white unitard designed by artist Henri Matisse. Though the costume was not a problem for Parisian audiences, it was considered indecent by Londoners and was modified with a chiffon overlayer.

Three years later, the ballet *Ode* was commissioned by Diaghilev for the Ballets Russes. The "strange, inventive" sets were complemented by a range of costumes, all designed by the Surrealist artist Pavel Tchelitchew. Most extraordinary were the sleek, ultramodern white leotards, tights, and head coverings that were worn not by young dancers as in *Le Chant du Rossignol* but by several mature ballerinas. One of them, Alexandra Danilova, felt naked in the rather scandalous costume. But it was highly effective on her and another dancer, Felia Doubrovska, who enhanced the concept of modern ballet with her long, lean frame and beautiful, well-proportioned legs and feet.

disappears; the flabby parts are stretched and are distributed harmoniously; individual isolated defects, such as redness and even—horror of horrors—the body's hairiness, vanish." He concluded that in silk tights, "the leg acquires its fullest possible perfection. The magnificent works of Greek sculpture always represented the human form free of all blemishes, defects and peculiarities."[15] The modern affinity for classical sculpture and the greater exposure of the human body during the classical revival in the arts of the 1910s–1930s may help explain why the leotard moved from ballet class to the stage, and eventually to the fashion arena.

The trend toward pared-down costumes took hold even in Russia after the revolution, as Volynsky observed: "Women are arrayed in tricot, to which they adapt as if it were their own second skin. They constantly need the stimulating chill created by the touch of the silk fabric against their naked body. Here everything is made level and smooth, is tight fitting and flattened out. The individual details—such as isolated roundness, depressions, angles, and blemishes—have disappeared, and a certain universal and idealized model of the individual body is created. From the earliest years of work in rehearsal and onstage, the artist needs to learn to look at

Ballets Russes ballerina Felia Doubrovska in Léonide Massine's *Ode,* 1928. Costumes by Pavel Tchelitchew.

DANSKIN ✕ NOT JUST FOR DANCING.™

FROM A.M. EXERCISING TO P.M. PARTYING, DANSKIN® LEOTARDS ARE PERFECT 24 HOURS A DAY. CHOOSE FROM STYLES LIKE THIS PINCH FRONT, GATHERED SHOULDER LEOTARD IN OUR OWN SHIMMERY, FIGURE FLATTERING, TRIMSKIN™ FABRIC; AVAILABLE IN TWELVE SPARKLING COLORS. AT FINE STORES EVERYWEAR.

For stores, see page 277

DANSKIN®

What made August's efforts so successful was a blend of corporate support, design ingenuity (including her use of Lycra spandex, then a cutting-edge material), correctly assessing the needs of a growing number of working and health-conscious women, and reliance on dance as a primary source of inspiration, specifically the worldwide popularity of ballet. The company's catchy slogan—"Danskin, not just for dancing"—perfectly described August's appropriation of the leotard, which moved from the ballet class to the stage, and finally to the street.

Advising August was Rebecca Wright, a soloist at American Ballet Theatre. Described as pert and sunny, Wright had speed, lightness, and virtuoso technique. In the introduction to August's 1981 book, *The Complete Bonnie August Dressthin System*, the designer credits Wright with

himself from the world's point of view."[16] This voyeuristic and somewhat fetishistic take on ballet tights could easily have been applied to fashion.

The intersection between fashion and streamlined dancewear reached its apogee during the 1970s. Their fusion was as relevant to classical ballet as it was to the discotheque, and much of the commercial credit for this phenomenon can be attributed to Bonnie August. Born in 1948, the American fashion creator became the design director of Danskin, Inc., then the largest manufacturer of leotards and dancewear in the United States (and possibly the world). By 1978, four years after August started to work at Danskin, the company's sales more than doubled, to over $90,000,000 annually. So great was August's impact that Danskin won a special Coty Award that year.

DANSKINS ARE NOT JUST FOR DANCING

THEY'RE FOR SLEEK, SEXY, AND CURVY PEOPLE WHO KNOW HOW TO SPEAK DANSKIN'S BODY LANGUAGE BEAUTIFULLY AND WANT TO ADD LOTS OF MILEAGE TO THEIR WARDROBES. WHILE DANSKIN'S FREESTYLE LEOTARD/SWIMSUITS ARE MADE FOR THE POOL AND DANCE STUDIO, THEY'RE PERFECT FOR EVENING WHEN PAIRED WITH A LONG SKIRT. MADE OF A SCINTILLATING BLEND OF ANTRON® NYLON AND LYCRA® SPANDEX, IN SIZES S, M, L, ABOUT 13.50. AT FINE STORES OR WRITE FOR BROCHURE V5, DANSKIN, INC., 1114 AVENUE OF THE AMERICAS, NEW YORK, N.Y. 10036.

DANSKIN®

Danskin advertisements, 1982 (left) and 1976 (right).

showing her tricks that dancers use to elongate their leg lines. August incorporated Wright's ideas and insights into her fashion designs.

Images of ballerinas as models continued during the 1970s, but at a reduced pace. One of the most famous was a perfume ad featuring Suzanne Farrell, one of Balanchine's final muses. Although she was a NYCB fixture for most of her career, Farrell took a hiatus when Balanchine became

enraged over her 1969 marriage to fellow NYCB dancer Paul Mejia. The groom was prohibited from dancing, prompting the couple to quit and leave New York. Soon thereafter, they began to dance with Maurice Béjart's Ballet du XXe Siècle. In 1972, while performing with that company in Paris, Farrell was tapped by Robert Ricci, head of the fashion house of Nina Ricci, to be the poster girl for its signature fragrance, L'Air du Temps. Although Farrell did not think she could "compete with the beautiful crystal doves that graced the top of the bottle,"[17] the softly focused image of her by David Hamilton "whirling in white chiffon, her ethereal reach longer than her pinwheeling skirt"[18] appeared frequently in an array of magazines and newspapers throughout the decade.

Another of the era's greatest ballerinas, Gelsey Kirkland, was featured in a dual portrait with fellow New York City Ballet dancer Judith Fugate in the December 1970 issue of *Harper's Bazaar*. The young women, photographed by Chris von Wangenheim, reflected the fashionable tastes with their wistful, fairy-like looks, tinged with a hint of rock 'n' roll edginess. After she left NYCB and moved to American Ballet Theatre, Kirkland appeared in a four-page editorial spread in *Vogue*'s December 1975 issue. Rather than presenting her in an array of high-fashion garments, the piece focused on her artistic accomplishments. In one photo she wears a costume; another is a close-up of her face. Kirkland was not a fashion-publication mainstay, but her physique conformed to the increasingly skinny body type that dominated both ballet and fashion. In her candid autobiography, *Dancing on My Grave*, Kirkland recounts her harrowing struggles with anorexia, bulimia, and cocaine addiction—diseases that nearly killed her.

Farrell and Kirkland may not have had as strong an impact on fashion as Kent and Paul had a decade earlier, but their brushes with fashion illustrated the continued cultural importance of ballet. Even though some leading fashion photographers such as Arthur Elgort ardently embraced ballet in the 1970s—a French *Vogue* fashion spread of his featured NYCB's Carole Divet swathed in Russian lynx—ballerinas' appearances in fashion magazines were increasingly rare. And the ballerina's signature costume no longer influenced designers the way it had during the mid-century.

ABOVE: NYCB ballerinas Gelsey Kirkland and Judith Fugate. *Harper's Bazaar*, December 1970.
OPPOSITE: NYCB ballerina Carole Divet modeling a lynx coat. French *Vogue*, 1980.

CONCLUSION

PATRICIA MEARS

The early years of the twentieth century saw the rise of the ballerina as an influential cultural figure. Any remaining stigma of her marginal position in society was all but erased during the interwar years, and her iconic costume—the tutu—inspired an entirely new style of evening dress, one that dominated mid-century fashion. By the 1980s, the tutu had become a pop-culture fixture, worn by such stars as Sarah Jessica Parker in the opening credits of the hit television series *Sex and the City*, and Madonna during the early years of her career, albeit in a decidedly punk way.

Yet in the minds of many fans and critics who became infatuated with ballet at mid-century, today's productions and dancers lack the artistry and urgency that had made classical dance special and significant. Ballet's glamour and creativity, so vital during the hardships of the Depression, World War II, and the Cold War, have waned, in large part because the great figures who gave rise to balletomania have passed. If the careers of Sergei Diaghilev and Anna Pavlova ignited the passion for ballet in the West, the death of George Balanchine in 1983 marked a dimming of this once bright flame.

Nevertheless, fashion in the 1980s continued to be influenced by ballet attire. Donna Karan in New York and Azzedine Alaia in Paris, for example, gave the leotard an increasingly important role in the world of high fashion. Karan's "bodysuit" was a luxurious foundation marketed toward the growing number of female professionals and businesswomen who were interested in donning something more distinctive than slightly feminized versions of men's suits. Made of knitted cashmere, Karan's bodysuits, topped with matching wrap skirts that snugly swathed the female body, served as a powerful and sexy base for her office-ready, beautifully tailored blazers and coats. Alaia, too, designed a range of fitted bodysuits and similarly cut dresses. These superbly made knits were not only for women climbing the corporate

NYCB ballerina Lauren Lovette in Maggie Norris's "Angelique" gold-embroidered corset and tulle skirt, 2012.

LEFT: Philanthropist
Judith-Ann Corrente's
evening ensemble
with a striped-cotton
and lace top and
silk gingham skirt
by Geoffrey Beene,
1987–88.
OPPOSITE: Philanthropist
Lauren Leichtman's
evening dress with a
sequined bodice and
a pink plaid and gauze
skirt by Geoffrey Beene,
ca. 1985.

ladder; they were assertive, body-conscious clothing for the fashion-forward consumer.

Another leading designer who appropriated balletic elements was Geoffrey Beene. A master of mixing color, texture, and pattern, as well as a perfectionist whose clothing was exquisitely constructed and finished, Beene was as committed to movement and function as he was to beauty and quality. Between 1991 and 1994, he routinely incorporated ballet dancers into his his biannual fashion shows. For one show, students from the School of American Ballet, NYCB's official training institute, modeled Beene's signature knitted jumpsuits while performing ballet movements. He also presented oversized drawings and photographs of ballerinas wearing that season's collection. Perhaps it is not surprising that Beene drew inspiration from ballet attire and tapped dancers for his shows, as he was a friend of Lincoln Kirstein's and a board member of American Ballet Theatre.

If Karan, Alaia, and Beene designed modern takes on movement-oriented dancewear, others occasionally crafted evening ensembles that harked back to Romantic-era ballet tutus. One example is New York–based designer Carolyne Roehm's gold lace confection with matching pointe shoe–style slippers. A disciple of Oscar de la Renta, Roehm was the wife of billionaire financier Henry Kravis. She became a star of Manhattan's Nouvelle Society, hosting lavish parties and acquiring blue-chip real estate properties and works of art with her husband, while running her eponymous fashion house. A photo of Roehm modeling the dress appeared in many publications in 1990, thus illustrating the continued desire of some women to assume the ballerina's guise.

Fashion's opulence could also be found on the ballet stage. In 1988 couturier Christian Lacroix designed the costumes for American Ballet Theatre's revival of Léonide Massine's 1938 *Gaîté Parisienne*. Originally performed by the Ballet Russe de Monte Carlo, it is a high-spirited work set during France's Second Empire with music by Jacques Offenbach. Lacroix brilliantly captured the ballet's zest and verve with his signature blend of eye-popping color and frenetic patterns. A number of critics contended that the costumes were the best part of the production. Despite these

ABOVE: Black wool jersey jumpsuit with brown leather harness by Geoffrey Beene, 1995.
OPPOSITE: NYCB dancer Deanna McBrearty modeling a jumpsuit by Geoffrey Beene, 1993.

OPPOSITE: Gold and pink metallic tulle and lace evening dress with matching shoes by Carolyne Roehm, 1990.
ABOVE: Advertisement featuring designer Carolyne Roehm modeling her evening dress, 1990.

Carole Divet Harting's yellow silk evening dress designed by Alber Elbaz for Lanvin, summer 2008.
OPPOSITE: Haute couture black and pink silk net evening dress with red silk satin ribbon by Christian Lacroix, ca. 1990.

notable efforts, however, ballet's impact on fashion continued to be rather scattershot throughout the 1980s and 1990s.

Balletic influence on high fashion began to increase in the early years of the new millenium. One example exemplfying this revival is a dress from the autumn/winter 2003 collection of Behnaz Sarafpour. Like a number of young designers at the time, she embraced a return to ladylike dressing. Inspired by mid-century couture and classical ballet, Sarafpour's dress was a hit because, as noted in "The School of Tulle," an article about the collection, it not only invoked the "elegance of Swan Lake tutus" but was also modern, capturing "the spirit of the ballerinas who, when work is over, like the dance floor as much as the stage."[1] The sensitive blend of then-and-now may have come from Sarafpour's own ballet experience; she took classes at the Joffrey Ballet School in New York and worked on costumes by Isaac Mizrahi that were commissioned by American Ballet Theatre[2] when she was his assistant in the 1990s. Sarafpour's 2003 design—with its fitted, gold-brocaded bodice and calf-length white tulle skirt—garnered tremendous press and was named one the year's best dresses by *People* magazine. Worn by actress Selma Blair to the Metropolitan Museum of Art's Costume Institute Gala that May, the dress regalvanized fashion's interest in ballerina attire.

Classical ballet has recently been undergoing something of a global resurgence. Powerhouse centers like Russia, as well as countries in Asia and Latin America, have been producing a new crop of star dancers and a new generation of ballet fans. Concurrently, ballet's influence on fashion in the Far East has also been on the rise. One highly publicized example was Japanese designer Rei Kawakubo's Biker + Ballerina collection, created for the spring/summer 2005 ready-to-wear season. Often described as the most intellectually and conceptually talented fashion designer in the world, Kawakubo (who works under the label Comme des Garçons), along with her compatriot Yohji Yamamoto, took the fashion world by storm in the early 1980s with her dark, deconstructed, and body-obfuscating clothes.

For her 2005 collection, Kawakubo paired her heavy black leather jackets with actual tutus from a British dance company for the runway presentation. Later, for the retail market, the tutus were replaced by ballet-inspired skirts made of candy-pink-colored synthetics. Kawakubo inverted fashion norms and erased compatible gender elements by pairing the aggressive masculine leather jacket with overtly feminine dance skirts. Yet the result was a surprisingly cohesive visual statement. Complementing the outfits were ballet-style flat shoes made by the French manufacturer Repetto, with whom she collaborated. But instead of resembling a soft dance slipper, Kawakubo's version was based on the boxy-toed pointe shoe.

The Japanese shoe designer Noritaka Tatehana created an extreme version of the ballerina's pointe shoe for Lady Gaga in 2011. Featured in her *Marry the Night* video, the appropriately named Lady Pointe shoe measures an extraordinary eighteen inches from top to toe. The accessory's obvious fetishistic appeal was further enhanced when paired with Gaga's balletic costume, made from latex.

Like women's high-fashion shoes, ballet slippers have been festish objects for centuries. As outlandish shoe design reached its apex in the early 2000s, creators such as Paris-based Christian Louboutin took the idea to new extremes. Unlike Tatehana, whose Lady Pointe shoes echoed the chopine—the blocky platform-style shoe worn by sixteenth-century Venetian courtesans—Louboutin took his cue from actual fetish boots of the Belle Époque. In 2007 he mounted a photography exhibition with film director David Lynch entitled *Fetish*. Photographs of performers from the famed Parisian cabaret Le Crazy Horse modeled an array of extreme designs, including Louboutin's own Fetish Ballerine. Made of black patent leather with his signature red sole, it clearly resembled a pointe shoe but with the addition of an eight-inch stiletto heel. Louboutin noted that this classical ballet shoe is the ultimate heel, one that "makes dancers closer than any other woman to the sky, closer to heaven!"[3] New York-based couturier Victor de Souza paired his version (made from an actual pointe shoe) with his ruffled tulle evening dress in 2016.

The rekindled interest in classical dance is due in part to the increasing diversity of these artist athletes (as they are now called), both ethnically and physically. The lack of ethnic diversity in the ballet world has been a hot topic for the past several years, especially in the United States. American Ballet

NYCB ballerina Lauren Lovette in a tulle and brocaded evening dress by Behnaz Sarafpour, autumn 2003.

ABOVE: "Biker Ballerina" leather jacket and synthetic tulle and chiffon skirt by Rei Kawakubo for Comme des Garçons, spring/summer 2005.

OPPOSITE: Pink leather heelless platform Lady Pointe shoes originally designed for Lady Gaga by Noritaka Tatehana, 2012.

LEFT: Black patent
leather Fetish Ballerine
shoes by Christian
Louboutin, 2014.
OPPOSITE: NYCB ballerina
Lauren Lovette wearing
black ballerina shoes by
Victor de Souza, 2016.

Theatre reaped tremendous publicity in 2016, when Misty Copeland became its first African American woman to be promoted to principal dancer—the highest rank. Copeland and her supporters attribute the lack of diversity in the ballet world primarily to the scarcity of opportunities for black dancers. But Copeland, curvy and muscular, is also among an elite group of ballerinas who have been pushing for greater body diversity. NYCB dancers—from the solidly athletic Ashley Bouder to the willowy bombshell Lauren Lovette—dance alongside leggy thoroughbreds such as Maria Kowroski. Interestingly, today's varied spectrum of dancers is similar to the highly individualized roster of modern ballet pioneers dancing in New York during the 1940s and 1950s.

Other contributions to the revived popularity of ballet include films such as *Black Swan*, released in 2010. A number of the movie's costumes, designed by the California sister duo Kate and Laura Mulleavy, who work under the label Rodarte, garnered considerable press and helped to rekindle interest in and deepen the connection between ballet and fashion. Former NYCB dancer and current fitness guru Mary Helen Bowers trained *Black Swan* stars Natalie Portman and Mila Kunis before taking on Kristina O'Neill, a leading fashion editor, as a client. Carine Roitfeld, another fashion editor, not only takes ballet classes but also often features dancers in her magazine, *CR Fashion Book*. In 2011 mainstream fashion firm J. Crew photographed its bestselling cashmere sweaters on dozens of students at the Vaganova Academy, the school of the Mariinsky Ballet, for its printed catalogue and website.

The number of leading dance companies that commission fashion designers to create new costumes has been on the rise since the beginning of the twenty-first century. The English National Ballet, for instance, engaged Karl Lagerfeld to design a tutu for a revival of Anna Pavlova's *The Dying Swan* solo. Though beautiful, the costume's high neckline (basically a feather-covered turtleneck) was not wholly successful, as it restricted the dancer's ability to evoke the essence of a bird noted for its long, sinuous, and flexible neck.

At the forefront of this phenomenon is New York City Ballet. Spearheaded by NYCB's prominent board member Sarah Jessica Parker, the company's annual fall gala features several new works by young choreographers, each of whom is paired with a leading fashion designer. Since the inception of this tradition in 2012, the list of prominent designers has included Valentino, Stella McCartney, Gilles Mendel, Thom Browne, Sarah Burton for Alexander McQueen, and Dries Van Noten. Thanks to the efforts of the company's director of costume, Marc Happel, radical fashion concepts are honed and crafted to meet the needs of dancers and choreographers alike.

Vintage ballet-related objects have also grown in popularity in recent years. After falling out of favor for decades, Van Cleef & Arpels' ballerina brooches now sell for record prices at auction. In 2018 a pin and matching ear clips sold for more than $300,000. Later that year, two dozen jewels from the collection of dancers Zizi Jeanmaire and Roland Petit netted nearly $635,000, more than double the estimates.

Sadly, ballet is not immune to ugly incidents that defame the beautiful art form. One of the most notorious and frightening events occurred on January 17, 2013, when the artistic director of the Bolshoi Ballet, Sergei Filin, was attacked with acid in Moscow. He suffered third-degree burns to his face and neck and lost sight in one eye despite numerous operations. The attackers were hired by one of the company's soloists, Pavel Dmitrichenko, after a lengthy period of infighting over casting decisions and other perceived inequities. More recent controversies include allegations of sexual misconduct by male members of companies ranging from the Royal Winnipeg Ballet to the New York City Ballet.

These scandalous stories are certainly not unique to ballet or any of the arts, for that matter. Today's dancers must face them, as they must cope with a plethora of new, rapid-fire changes, such as a world driven by, and saturated with, social-media images and information. Many young dancers and fashion designers alike are meeting these challenges with the same energy and vision that propelled their predecessors to greatness decades ago. And, by confronting issues that rupture the status quo, ballet and fashion will change and grow, hopefully together. It took two-and-a-half centuries for fashion to appreciate and appropriate the beauty and accoutrements of the ballerina. Let us hope their continued alliance will sustain them both in the years to come.

NYCB ballerina Lauren Lovette.

NOTES

INTRODUCTION

1   Lincoln Kirstein, "Ballet," *Vogue*, November 1, 1933, 29.

2   *Vogue*, September 1, 1937, 75.

CROWN JEWELS

1   Mary Clarke and Clement Crisp, *Ballerina: The Art of Women in Classical Ballet* (Princeton, NJ: Princeton Book Company Publishers, 1988), 7.

2   Elizabeth Kendall, *Balanchine & the Lost Muse: Revolution and the Making of a Choreographer* (New York: Oxford University Press, 2013), 75.

3   Lincoln Kirstein, "Ballet Alphabet" (1939), in *Ballet: Bias and Belief* (New York: Dance Horizons, 1983), 304.

4   Quoted in David Daniel, "Exits, Dancing," *Vanity Fair*, March 1987, 117.

5   Arnold L. Haskell, *Ballet: A Complete Guide to Appreciation* (Harmondsworth, Middlesex, UK: Penguin Books Limited, 1938), 18.

6   Cyril Beaumont, *The Ballet Called Giselle* (1944; repr. Hampshire, UK: Dance Books, 2011), 16.

7   André Levinson, *Marie Taglioni*, trans. Cyril W. Beaumont (1930; repr. Hampshire, UK: Noverre Press, 2014), 93.

8   Théophile Gautier, *The Romantic Ballet as Seen by Théophile Gautier, 1837–1848*, trans. Cyril W. Beaumont (New York: Books for Libraries, 1980), 73.

9   Deirdre Kelly, *Ballerina* (Vancouver, Canada: Greystone Books, 2012), 79–89.

10 Gelsey Kirkland and Greg Lawrence, *Dancing on My Grave* (New York: Doubleday & Company, 1986), 154–55.

11 Mary Clarke and Clement Crisp, *Ballerina: The Art of Women in Classical Ballet*, (Trenton, NJ: Princeton Book Company, 1989), 9.

12 The title of the sixth Cluny unicorn tapestry—*À Mon Seul Désir*—has been translated a number of ways, but the two most common translations are "To my sole desire" and "According to my desire alone." Still debated to this day is the question of whether the woman in the tapestry is taking the necklace from, or returning it to, the jewel box. The first interpretation sees the necklace as a symbol of love for the woman; the second suggests a renunciation of passion—this woman's power of free will. Certainly Balanchine, who was in love with Suzanne Farrell when he choreographed *Jewels*, and made "Diamonds" for her, was acting on the first interpretation. Farrell, a ballerina who was always beyond reach, exemplifies the second interpretation.

FASHION AND DANCE COSTUME IN THE NINETEENTH CENTURY

1   Wilhelm [Charles William Pitcher], "Art in the Theatre. Art in the Ballet, Part 1," *Magazine of Art*, vol, 18, 1985, 14; abridged in Russell Jackson, *Victorian Theatre: The Theatre in Its Time* (London: Black, 1989), 227–34.

2   "A Chat with Costumier Wilhelm at Home," *Sketch*, March 8, 1893, 343–44.

3   The case attracted newspapers as far away as the *New Zealand Evening Post*, July 15, 1905.

4   Theodore Wolff, "The Victory of the Tutu," manuscript in the collection of Ivor Guest at the V&A.

5   "Bettina de Sortis," *Daily Graphic*, February 14, 1891.

6   Lillian Moore, *Practice Clothes – Then and Now* (Capezio, n.d.), unpaginated.

7   Ivor Guest, "The Genesis of *La Sylphide*," in Marian Smith, ed., *La Sylphide: Paris 1832 and Beyond* (Alton, Hampshire, UK: Dance Books, 2012), 8.

8   *The Era*, December 23, 1877.

9   *Journal des Débats*, August 24, 1832.

10 Athol Mayhew, "The Building of a Ballet," *The Idler*, August 1892, 60–69.

11 Alicia Markova, Foreword, in Roy Strong et al., *Designing for the Dancer* (London: Elron Press, 1981).

12 Crinolines could be worn by dancers performing mime roles or stately dances. In a private collection, a costume design by Wilhelm for the second tableau of *Versailles* (1892) at the Empire—a Louis XIV-period panniered floor-length gown—is annotated "with crinolines also please."

13 Ivor Guest, *The Divine Virginia: A Biography of Virginia Zucchi* (New York: Dekker, 1977), 83–84.

TAGLIONI AND PAVLOVA: MAKINGS OF THE MODERN BALLERINA

1   Lynn Garafola, ed., *Rethinking the Sylph: New Perspectives on Romantic Ballet* (Middletown, CT: Wesleyan University Press, 1997), 1–2.

2   Caitlyn Lehmann, "La Syl-Fever: How Marie Taglioni and La Sylphide Took 19th-Century Popular Culture by Storm," August 7, 2013, The Australian Ballet online.

3   Ibid.

4   Ibid.

5   Pierer's Universal-Lexikon, Bd. 17, p. 205 (Altenburg, 1863), quoted by Muns, woormaling.ndernadsmusiekinsituut.nl

6 Lehmann, "La Syl-Fever."

7 Judith Chazin-Bennahum, *The Lure of Perfection: Fashion and Ballet, 1780–1830* (New York: Routledge, 2005), 172–73. It should be noted that this image was not correctly cited and could not be located.

8 April Calahan, *Fashion Plates: 150 Years of Style* (New Haven and London: Yale University Press, 2015), 160–61.

9 Tamara Karsavina, *Theatre Street: The Reminiscences of Tamara Karsavina* (London: Dance Books, 1981), 83.

10 Mathilde Kschessinska, *Dancing in Petersburg: The Memoirs of Kschessinska* (London: Gollancz, 1960), 133.

11 Keith Money, *Anna Pavlova: Her Life and Art* (New York: Alfred A. Knopf), 1982.

12 Julie Kavanagh, *Secret Muses: The Life of Frederick Ashton* (New York: Pantheon Books, 1996), 3.

13 Ibid., 4.

BALLET AND COUTURE IN THE MID-CENTURY

1 Joan Acocella, "Fifty Shades: Alexei Ratmansky Stages 'The Sleeping Beauty,'" *The New Yorker*, June 1, 2015, online.

2 Julie Kavanagh, *Secret Muses: The Life of Frederick Ashton*, 73.

3 Karl Lagerfeld, in the film *Chanel, Chanel*, RM Arts, 1986.

4 Lynn Garafola, "Les Soirées de Paris," in Milo Keynes, *Lydia Lopokova* (New York: Saint Martin's Press, 1983), 97.

5 Ibid.

6 "Dancer Sues for 100,000," *New York Tribune*, August 2, 1921, 5. MFIT search, newspapers.com.

7 Sono Osato, interview with author, July 2017. At the time of the interview, the former dancer was nearly ninety-eight years old. She was not uniformly coherent throughout the exchange, but when she was lucid, her recollections were logical and confirmed many of the suppositions presented to her.

8 *Harper's Bazaar*, May 1938, 78.

9 *Vogue*, September 15, 1938, 70.

10 Toni Bentley, *Costumes by Karinska* (New York: Harry N. Abrams, 1995), 105.

11 This dress was so popular that it appeared in at least two other fashion editorials, including one in *Harper's Bazaar*. Another version was modeled by British ballerina June Brae, who posed with Frederick Ashton on the set of his latest work, *Nocturne*, for British *Vogue*.

12 Joan Acocella, "Local Hero: Edward Villella's Miami City Ballet Come to Manhattan," *The New Yorker*, February 9, 2009, online.

13 *Vogue*, October 15, 1936, 86–87.

14 Bentley, *Costumes by Karinska*, 34.

15 Elizabeth Ann Coleman, *The Genius of Charles James* (New York: Henry Holt & Co, 1982), 14–15.

16 Margot Fonteyn, *Autobiography* (London: W. H. Allen, 1975), 101.

17 Rosemary Harden, "Margot Fonteyn and Fashion Designers in the 1940s," *Costume*, vol. 44 (May 2010): 96, 99–100.

18 Joy Williams also modeled in New York before and after her time in France. Her first appearance in a fashion magazine was in the May 1944 issue of *Glamour*. Immediately after the war, she was photographed with leading models such as Maxime de la Falaise. The dancer confirmed that she and other ballet professionals were not paid for their modeling efforts.

19 Fini painted Williams again in 1955, after her marriage and retirement from ballet. Entitled *La Fée*, this solo portrait depicts the former dancer in a white gown holding the same prickly wooden staff seen in the portrait with Fonteyn.

20 Eisenhower's press secretary, James C. Hagerty, a serious ballet fan, made frequent trips from D.C. to New York to watch Tallchief perform. At the time, the White House was striving for cultural outreach to Moscow, and a goodwill dance tour to the Soviet Union was suggested. Although American Ballet Theatre made the trip, the State Department wanted Tallchief, still with New York City Ballet, to go along. Balanchine consented, and off she went.

21 Maria Tallchief with Larry Kaplan, *Maria Tallchief: America's Prima Ballerina* (New York: Henry Holt, 1997).

22 Ibid., p.66.

23 Richard Buckle, *Modern Ballet Design: A Picture-book with Notes* (London: Adam and Charles Black, 1955), 78.

24 Bernard Taper, *Balanchine: A Biography with a New Epilogue* (Berkeley, CA: University of California Press, 1996), 426.

25 Gérard-Julien Salvy, *Pierre Balmain* (Paris: Les Éditions du Regard, 1995), 95.

26 Keith Money, *Fonteyn: The Making of a Legend* (New York: William Morrow and Company, 1974), 34.

27 Dilys E. Blum, *Shocking!: The Art and Fashion of Schiaparelli* (Philadelphia: Philadelphia Museum of Art, 2003), 44–45.

28 Laura Jacobs, "Tchaikovsky at the Millennium," *New Criterion*, vol. 18 (September 1999), 26.

29 *Harper's Bazaar*, April 1944, 10.

30 Laura Jacobs, "The Balanchine Tapestries," *Ballet Review*, Summer 2008, 27.

ENTER THE BALLERINA: MARGOT FONTEYN AND FASHION, 1930S–1960S

1   Programme header, The Royal Ballet, 2018.

2   *The Sleeping Beauty* (1946). Choreography by Marius Petipa, music by Piotr Ilich Tchaikovsky, sets and costumes by Oliver Messel.

3   The hat is in the collection of the Fashion Museum Bath (BATMC I.12.285).

4   Lesley Barrett, "The Amazing Margot Fonteyn," unknown magazine, 1966.

5   Dame Margot Fonteyn de Arias CBE was born Margaret Evelyn Hookham, also known as Peggy, and adopted her first stage name, Margot Fontes, in 1934, changing it to Margot Fonteyn by 1936. She called herself Margot Fonteyn de Arias, and was also referred to as Madame or Mrs. Roberto de Arias after she married in 1955. She was made a Dame Commander of the Order of the British Empire in 1956.

6   Letter, Margot Fonteyn to Harry W. Yoxall, February 14, 1940.

7   William Chappell, *Fonteyn: Impressions of a Ballerina* (London: Spring Books, 1950), 84.

8   Margot Fonteyn, *Autobiography* (London: W. H. Allen, 1975), 118.

9   *Façade* (1935). Choreography by Frederick Ashton, music by William Walton, scenery and costumes by John Armstrong.

10   "New Ballet at Sadler's Wells," *Daily News Chronicle*, October 9, 1935.

11   The Vic-Wells Ballet was founded ca.1926 and became known as the Sadler's Wells Ballet in 1940. The company became the Royal Ballet by Royal Charter in 1956.

12   Margot Fonteyn's mother, Hilda Hookham, née Fontes, of mixed Irish and Brazilian ancestry, was familiarly known as the Black Queen.

13   "Shanghai Girl Does Well in London," *Shanghai Times*, May 24, 1935.

14   *Sketch*, January 20, 1937, 133.

15   British *Vogue*, June 1944.

16   "Pas de Deux," British *Vogue*, April 1937.

17   *Tatler*, May 28, 1941.

18   British *Vogue*, June 1944, 46.

19   British *Vogue*, June 1943.

20   *Les Demoiselles de la Nuit* (1948). Choreography by Roland Petit, music by Jean Françaix, libretto by Jean Anouilh, sets and costumes by Leonor Fini.

21   Fonteyn, *Autobiography*, 115.

22   Fonteyn's "Goemon" coat is now in the collection at the Fashion Museum Bath (BATMC I.06.127).

23   *Femina*, October 1948.

24   "Paris Styles," *Yorkshire Evening News*, September 17, 1949.

25   *The Ambassador* was established by Hans and Elsbeth Juda in 1946. Hans was managing editor and proprietor; Elsbeth was photographer, working under the name "Jay." The magazine was a key press and marketing medium for the British clothing and textile industries struggling to reassert exports in a global marketplace after depleted sales during and after World War II.

26   Barbara Wace, "Meet Margot Fonteyn," unknown publication, 1949.

27   *Evening News*, September 23, 1949.

28   The tour ran from October 9 to December 11, 1949. It included four weeks at the Metropolitan Opera House in New York, followed by Washington, D.C., Richmond, Virginia, Philadelphia, Chicago, East Lansing, Michigan, and the Canadian cities of Toronto, Ottawa, and Montreal.

29   "The Ballet Wears British," *Picture Post*, September 10, 1949.

30   The Incorporated Society of London Fashion Designers was founded in 1941 as an organization of couturiers with the aim of promoting the British fashion and textile industry, particularly for export.

31   Minutes of Incorporated Society of London Fashion Designers, June 23, 1949.

32   Ibid.

33   Violetta Elvin's name is crossed out twice, and substituted, in handwriting, by that of Ninette de Valois.

34   David Webster was General Administrator of Covent Garden.

35   Minutes of Incorporated Society of London Fashion Designers, July 6, 1949.

36   Moira Shearer (1926–2006), star of *The Red Shoes* (1948), also featured widely in the pre-tour publicity.

37   This was Fonteyn's "travel" suit by Michael Sherard (1910–1998).

38   *Bridlington Free Press*, August 20, 1949.

39   The suit is in the collection of the Fashion Museum Bath (BATMC I.24.43 & A).

40   *Sphere*, December 11, 1948. Fonteyn is shown with her leg in a cast. *Daily Graphic*, August 10, 1949. Fonteyn is shown wearing the suit at Hardy Amies's couture house.

41   *Vogue*, October 15, 1948.

42   Fonteyn is pictured with ballerinas Beryl Grey (b. 1927) and Pamela May (1917–2005), wearing ensembles by Victor Stiebel and Charles Creed, respectively.

43   Invitation, October 7, 1949.

44   British *Vogue*, October 1949, 86–87.

45 The evening dress is part of the collection at Fashion Museum Bath (BATMC I.09.898 & A).

46 "Ballet Tailpiece," *Truth*, October 21, 1949.

47 "Coloratura on Tiptoe," *Time*, November 14, 1949, 28.

48 The evening dress "Marigny" is in the collection of the Fashion Museum Bath (BATMC I.09.783 to C).

49 Mary Van Rensselaer Thayer, *Washington Post*, November 10, 1949.

50 An article in the *News Chronicle* on December, 12, 1949, quoted Sir John Anderson, Chairman of the Covent Garden Trust, who, when asked how much Sadler's Wells had earned on the tour "put it at 75,000 dollars, adding, 'We did not expect to make a profit.'" The company gave 74 performances, to 225,000 people. They transported 40 tons of scenery.

51 *Daily Mirror*, December 17, 1949.

52 *Daily Telegraph*, December 17, 1949.

53 Chappell, *Fonteyn: Impressions of a Ballerina*, 84.

54 *Picture Post*, November 16, 1950.

55 Biographical notes, prepared by Biddy Noal, July 1950.

56 "Debussy" is in the collection at the Fashion Museum Bath (BATMC I.09.338 to B).

57 U.K. examination board focusing on dance education and training.

58 *Evening Standard*, October 7, 1953.

59 A Panamanian lawyer and politician, often referred to as Tito, whom Fonteyn had first met in the 1930s.

60 *Firebird* (1954). Choreography by Michel Fokine, music by Igor Stravinsky, sets and costumes by Natalia Goncharova. Fonteyn premiered this production of the ballet in August 1954, first at the Edinburgh Festival and then at Covent Garden. She was coached by Tamara Karsavina, who had originated the title role for Sergei Diaghilev's Ballets Russes in 1910.

61 Horrockses, a British ready-to-wear firm known for printed cotton dresses, was founded in 1946 and was part of a much older cotton firm in Lancashire, England, which started production in the late eighteenth century.

62 Susan Small, a British ready-to-wear firm known for party dresses, was founded by Leslie Carr-Jones in the early 1940s.

63 "Margot Is Hostage," *Daily Sketch*, April 22,1959.

64 *Daily Mail*, April 25,1959.

65 "A Magnificent Entrance," *Manchester Guardian*, April 25, 1959.

66 Fonteyn, *Autobiography*, 246.

67 *Giselle* (1960). Choreography by Frederick Ashton, music by Adolphe Adam, sets and costumes by John Bailey. Fonteyn premiered this production of the ballet in September 1960 at the Metropolitan Opera House, New York.

68 "Dance and Dancers," April 1962, quoted in Meredith Daneman, *Margot Fonteyn* (London: Viking, 2004), 402.

69 Barrett, "The Amazing Margot Fonteyn," unknown publication.

70 The hat is part of the collection at the Fashion Museum Bath (BATMC I.12.433).

71 The dress is in the collection at the Fashion Museum Bath (BATMC I.09.846).

72 Unknown publication.

73 *Illustrated London News*, November 6, 1965.

74 The dress is in the collection at the Fashion Museum Bath (BATMC I.09.603).

75 Margot Fonteyn obituary, *Daily Telegraph*, February 22, 1991.

76 Anthony Dowell, Margot Fonteyn obituary, *Daily Telegraph*, February 22, 1991.

DRYADS OF WEST 55TH STREET

1 Joel Lobenthal, "A Conversation with Robert Barnett," *Ballet Review*, Winter 2013–14, 49.

2 Joel Lobenthal, *Wilde Times: Patricia Wilde, George Balanchine, and the Rise of New York City Ballet* (Lebanon, NH: ForeEdge/University Press of New England, 2016), 119.

3 Barbara Walczak, interview with author, December 2012.

4 Joel Lobenthal, *Radical Rags: Fashions of the Sixties* (New York Abbeville Press, 1990), 110.

5 Joel Lobenthal, "A Conversation with Nora White," *Ballet Review*, Summer 2015, 66.

6 Lobenthal, *Wilde Times*, 166.

7 John Taras, interview with author, December 1999.

8 Muriel Stuart, interview with author, December 1981.

9 Virginia Brooks, director, *Felia Doubrovska Remembered: From Diaghilev's Ballets Russes to Balanchine's School of American Ballet*, Brooks Dance Films and Video, 2008.

10 Joel Lobenthal, "A Conversation with Betty Nichols," *Ballet Review*, Fall 2013, 59.

11 Edith Le Clercq, interview with author, November 1981.

12 "Remembering Tanaquil Le Clercq," *Ballet Review*, Summer 2001, 50.

13 Lobenthal, "A Conversation with Robert Barnett," 42.

14 Thank you to the Jerome Robbins Rights Trust for permission to quote from the Le Clercq–Robbins correspondence here and throughout this essay.

15 Walczak interview, December 2012.

16 Deborah Jowitt, *Time and the Dancing Image* (New York: William Morrow, 1988), 268.

17 Holly Brubach, "Muse, Interrupted," *New York Times Magazine*, November 22, 1998, 64.

18 Walczak interview, December 2012.

19 B. H. Haggin, "Music," *The Nation*, March 26, 1955, 274.

20 Nancy Reynolds, *Repertory in Review: 40 Years of the New York City Ballet* (New York: Dial Press, 1977), 134.

21 Jonathan Watts, interview with author, March 2014.

22 Janice Cohen, interview with author, November 2017.

23 Lobenthal, "A Conversation with Robert Barnett," 49–50.

24 Francis Gadan and Robert Maillard, eds., *A Dictionary of Modern Ballet* (London: Methuen, 1959), 208.

25 Toni Bentley, *Costumes by Karinska* (New York: Harry N. Abrams, 1995), 130.

AMERICAN BALLET AND READY-TO-WEAR FASHION, 1940S–1950S

1 "Leotards: The Acrobats' Tights Make News This Year in College Fashions." *Life*, September 13, 1943.

2 A full-page photograph by Kollar of Markova in rehearsal clothing appears in the October 1938 issue of *Harper's Bazaar*, p. 86.

3 Claire McCardell, *What Shall I Wear?: The What, Where, When, and How Much of Fashion* (New York: Simon & Schuster, 1956).

4 *Harper's Bazaar*, July 1941, 44–45.

5 One pair of flats is recorded as having been inspired by a pair of shoes dating to 1800–1810 in the Brooklyn Museum's Design Lab, where McCardell was a member. Though it is not certain that McCardell herself designed these shoes, the style is very much in line with her work for the company.

6 Gay Pauley, "Vera Maxwell Becomes 'Museum Piece,'" *Times Daily*, December 11, 1980. Retrieved July 6, 2016, online at https://news.google.com/

7 Phyllis Magidson, quoted in Kohle Yohannan, *Valentina: American Couture and the Cult of Celebrity* (New York: Rizzoli, 2009), 15.

WAIFS AND MODS: BALLET AND FASHION, 1960S–1970S

1 All the information cited about the creation of the CFDA was taken from Eleanor Lambert's archives, now part of the Special Collection, housed in the Fashion Institute of Technology's Library. Included are thousands of letters, memoranda, programs, and other papers belonging to Lambert and the CFDA. In this quote, Lambert may have confused Balanchine's *Brahms-Schoenberg Quartet* with Robbins's *Goldberg Variations*.

2 Alastair Macaulay, "Frederick Ashton's Masterly Pas de Trois," *New York Times*, Oct. 14, 2015, online.

3 Laura Jacobs, *Celestial Bodies: How to Look at Ballet* (New York: Basic Books, 2018), 73.

4 Jennifer Homans, *Apollo's Angels: A History of Ballet* (New York: Random House, 2010), 383–86.

5 *Harper's Bazaar*, September 1959, 183.

6 Ibid., 182.

7 Ekaterina Trifonova, "Yves Saint Laurent and Russia: A love affair that continues to this day," August 1, 2016, Russia Beyond, https://www.rbth.com/multimedia/history/2016/08/01/yves-saint-laurent-and-russia-a-love-affair-that-continues-to-this-day_617065.

8 Allegra Kent, *Once a Dancer . . .: An Autobiography* (New York: St. Martin's Press, 1997), 117.

9 Allegra Kent, "Dance of the Muse," *Vogue*, October 2006, 130.

10 Ibid., 134.

11 Suzy Kalter, "Danskin Designer Bonnie August Has Got Almost Everybody Going Around in Next to Nothing," *People*, June 18, 1979.

12 Ibid.

13 Steve Ward, *Sawdust Sisterhood: How Circus Empowered Women* (Stroud, UK: Fonthill Media, 2016), 87.

14 Akim Volynsky, *Ballet's Magic Kingdom: Selected Writings on Dance in Russia, 1911–1925* (New Haven, CT, and London: Yale University Press, 2008), 104.

15 Ibid., 154.

16 Ibid.

17 Suzanne Farrell with Toni Bentley, *Holding On to the Air: An Autobiography* (New York: Summit Books, 1990), 207.

18 Laura Jacobs, "Dancing the Body Electric," *City Journal*, winter 2011, online.

CONCLUSION

1 Amy Larocca, "The School of Tulle," *New York*, September 22, 2003.

2 The ballet, *Brief Fling*, was choreographed by Twyla Tharp. It debuted at the Metropolitan Opera in New York in 1990.

3 Megan Gustashaw, "NSFT: Behold, Christian Louboutin's Insanely Amazing Ballerina Heels," June 29, 2011, https://www.glamour.com/story/how-much-would-you-pay-for-the.

Silk chiffon evening dresses by Jean Dessès, 1953–56.

SELECTED BIBLIOGRAPHY

BOOKS AND ARTICLES

The Archers (Michael Powell and Emeric Pressburger, producers and directors). *The Red Shoes*, United Kingdom, 1948.

August, Bonnie, with Ellen Count. *Complete Bonnie August Dressthin System*. New York: Rawson, Wade Publishers, 1981.

Balmain, Pierre. Balmain; *My Years and Seasons*. London: Cassell, 1964.

Beaumont, Cyril W. *The Vic-Wells Ballet*. London: C. W. Beaumont, 1935.

_____. *The Sadler's Wells Ballet*. London: C. W. Beaumont, 1946.

_____. *The Ballet Called Giselle*. London: C. W. Beaumont, 1944. Reprint, Hampshire, UK: Dance Books, 2011.

Bentley, Toni. *Costumes by Karinska*. New York: Harry N. Abrams, 1995.

Bloom, Julie. "New Costumes at City Ballet." *New York Times* online, May 10, 2012.

Blum, Dilys. *Shocking!: The Art and Fashion of Schiaparelli*. Philadelphia and New Haven, CT: Philadelphia Museum of Art and Yale University Press, 2003.

Buckle, Richard. *Modern Ballet Design: A Picture-Book with Notes*. London: Adam and Charles Black, 1955.

Breward, Christopher, and Claire Wilcox, eds. *The Ambassador Magazine: Promoting Post-War British Textiles and Fashion*. London: V&A Publishing, 2012.

Chaffee, George. "Three or Four Graces: A Centenary Salvo." *Dance Index*, vol. 3, nos. 9–11 (September–November 1944). https://archive.org/details/danceindexunse_20/page/n1

Chappell, William. *Fonteyn: Impressions of a Ballerina*. London: Spring Books, 1950.

Chazin-Bennahum, Judith. *The Lure of Perfection: Fashion and Ballet, 1780–1830*. New York and London: Routledge, 2005.

Christout, Marie-Françoise, and Fernande Bassan. "Les Ballets des Champs-Élysées: A Legendary Adventure." *Dance Chronicle*, vol. 27, no. 2 (2004), 157–98.

Clarke, Mary, and Clement Crisp. *Ballet: An Illustrated History*. New York: Universe Books, 1973.

_____. *Design for Ballet*. London: Cassell and Collier, Macmillan Publishers, 1978.

_____. *Ballerina: The Art of Women in Classical Ballet*. Princeton, NJ: Princeton Book Company Publishers, 1989.

Coleman, Elizabeth Ann. *The Genius of Charles James*. New York: The Brooklyn Museum and Holt, Rinehart and Winston, 1982.

Daneman, Meredith. *Margot Fonteyn: A Life*. New York: Penguin Books, 2005.

Danilova, Alexandra. *Choura: The Memoirs of Alexandra Danilova*. New York: Alfred A. Knopf, 1986.

de la Haye, Amy, and Edwina Ehrman, eds. *London Couture 1923–1975: British Luxury*. London: V&A Publishing, 2015.

de Valois, Ninette. *Come Dance with Me: A Memoir, 1898–1956*. Cleveland and New York: The World Publishing Co., 1957.

Dorris, George. "Dance and the New Opera War, 1906–1912." *Dance Chronicle*, vol. 32, no. 2 (2009), 195–262.

_____. "The Metropolitan Opera Ballet, Fresh Starts: Rosina Galli and the Ballets Russes, 1912–1917." *Dance Chronicle*, vol. 35. no. 2 (2012), 173–207.

Farrell, Suzanne, with Toni Bentley. *Holding On to the Air: An Autobiography*. New York: Summit Books, 1990.

Fisher, Jennifer. *Nutcracker Nation: How an Old World Ballet Became a Christmas Tradition in the New World*. New Haven, CT, and London: Yale University Press, 2003.

Fonteyn, Margot. *Autobiography*. London: W. H. Allen, 1975.

_____. *The Magic of Dance*. New York: Alfred A. Knopf, 1979.

Gadan, Francis, and Robert Maillard, eds. *A Dictionary of Modern Ballet*. London: Methuen, 1959.

Garafola, Lynn. "Les Soirées de Paris." In Milo Keynes, ed. *Lydia Lopokova*. New York: St. Martin's Press, 1982, 97–105.

_____, ed. *Rethinking the Sylph: New Perspectives on the Romantic Ballet*. Hanover, NH, and London: Wesleyan University Press and University Press of New England, 1997.

Garafola, Lynn, and Eric Foner, eds. *Dance for a City: Fifty Years of the New York City Ballet*. New York: Columbia University Press, 1999.

Garnier, Guillaume. *Pierre Balmain: 40 années de création*. Paris: Musée de La Mode et du Costume, 1985.

Pink silk chiffon and silk chiffon crepe evening dress by Madame Grès, 1969.

Gautier, Théophile. Translated by Cyril W. Beaumont. *The Romantic Ballet as Seen by Théophile Gautier, 1837–1848*. New York: Books for Libraries, 1980.

Goldschmidt, Hubert. "Marie Taglioni." *Ballet Review*, Summer 2018, 100–124.

Grey, Beryl. *Red Curtain Up*. New York: Dodd, Mead & Company, 1958.

Guest, Ivor. *The Divine Virginia: A Biography of Virginia Zucchi*. New York: Dekker, 1977.

_____. "The Genesis of *La Sylphide*." In Marian Smith, ed. *La Sylphide: Paris 1832 and Beyond*. Alton, Hampshire, UK: Dance Books, 2012.

Guillaume, Valérie. *Jacques Fath*. Paris: Éditions Paris Musées/Adam Biro, 1993.

Harden, Rosemary. "Margot Fonteyn and Fashion Designers of the 1940s." *Costume*, vol. 44, no. 1 (May 2010), 96–105.

Haskell, Arnold L. *Ballet: A Complete Guide to Appreciation, History, Aesthetics, Ballets, Dancers*. Harmondsworth, Middlesex, UK: Penguin Books, 1938.

_____. *Balletomania: The Story of an Obsession*. New York: Simon & Schuster, 1934.

Homans, Jennifer. *Apollo's Angels: A History of Ballet*. New York: Random House, 2010.

Jacobs, Laura. "Balanchine's Castle: On Jewels at the New York State Theater, Lincoln Center." *New Criterion*, March 1998.

_____. "Dancing the Body Electric: A Look Back at New York's 1970s Dance Boom." *City Journal*, winter 2011. https://www.city-journal.org/html/dancing-body-electric-13358.html.

_____. "The Balanchine Tapestries." *Ballet Review*, vol. 36, no. 2 (Summer 2008) 27–39.

_____. *Celestial Bodies: How to Look at Ballet*. New York: Basic Books, 2018.

Jowitt, Deborah. *Time and the Dancing Image*. New York: William Morrow, 1988.

Karsavina, Tamara. *Theatre Street: The Reminiscences of Tamara Karsavina*. London: Dance Books, 1981.

Kavanagh, Julie. *Secret Muses: The Life of Frederick Ashton*. New York: Pantheon, 1997.

Kelly, Deirdre. *Ballerina: Sex, Scandal, and Suffering Behind the Symbol of Perfection*. Vancouver, Canada: Greystone Books, 2012.

Kendall, Elizabeth. *Balanchine & the Lost Muse: Revolution and the Making of a Choreographer*. New York: Oxford University Press, 2013.

Kent, Allegra. *Once a Dancer . . . : An Autobiography*. New York: St. Martin's Press, 1997.

Kirkland, Gelsey. *Dancing on My Grave*. New York: Doubleday, 1986.

Kirstein, Lincoln. "Ballet." *Vogue*, November 1, 1933, 29.

_____. "Ballet Alphabet" (1939). In *Ballet: Bias and Belief*. New York: Dance Horizons, 1983.

_____. *Four Centuries of Ballet: Fifty Masterworks*. New York: Dover Publications, 1984.

Kochno, Boris. *Christian Bérard*. London: Thames & Hudson, 1988.

Kschessinska, Mathilde. Translated by Arnold Haskell. *Dancing in Petersburg: The Memoirs of Kschessinska*. London: Victor Gollancz, 1960.

Lehmann, Caitlyn. "La Syl-fever: How Marie Taglioni and La Sylphide Took 19th-Century Popular Culture by Storm," August 7, 2018. The Australian Ballet online. https://australianballet.com.au/behind-ballet/la-syl-fever

Levinson, André. Translated by Susan Cook Summer. *Ballet Old and New*. New York: Dance Horizons, 1982.

_____. *Marie Taglioni*. Translated by Cyril W. Beaumont. London: Imperial Society of Teachers of Dancing, 1930. Reprint, Hampshire, UK: Noverre Press, 2014.

Lobenthal, Joel. *Radical Rags: Fashions of the Sixties*. New York: Abbeville Press, 1990.

_____. *Alla Osipenko: Beauty and Resistance in Soviet Ballet*. New York and Oxford, UK: Oxford University Press, 2015.

_____. *Wilde Times: Patricia Wilde, George Balanchine, and the Rise of New York City Ballet*. Lebanon, NH: ForeEdge/University Press of New England, 2016.

Macaulay, Alastair. *Margot Fonteyn*. Stroud, Gloucestershire, UK: Sutton Publishing, 1998.

Money, Keith. *Fonteyn: The Making of a Legend*. New York: William Morrow, 1974.

_____. *Anna Pavlova: Her Life and Art*. New York: Alfred A. Knopf, 1982.

Morrison, Kirsty. *From Russia with Love*. Canberra: National Gallery of Australia, 1998.

Noble, Peter, ed. *British Ballet*. London: Skelton Robinson, 1949.

Osato, Sono. *Distant Dances*. New York: Alfred A. Knopf, 1980.

Payne, Charles. *American Ballet Theatre*. New York: Alfred A. Knopf, 1978.

Plisetskaya, Maya. Translated by Antonina W. Bouis. *I, Maya Plisetskaya*. New Haven, CT: Yale University Press, 2001.

Pritchard, Jane, and Geoffrey Marsh. *Diaghilev and the Ballets Russes 1909–1929*. Reprint, London: V&A Publishing, 2015.

Reade, Brian. *Ballet Designs and Illustrations 1581–1940*. London: Her Majesty's Stationery Office, 1967.

Reynolds, Nancy. *Repertory in Review: 40 Years of the New York City Ballet*. New York: Dial Press, 1977.

Salvy, Gerard-Julien. *Pierre Balmain*. Paris: Les Éditions du Regard, 1995.

Savignon, Jéromine. *Jacques Fath*. New York: Assouline Publishing, 2008.

Schouvaloff, Alexander. *The Art of Ballets Russes*. New Haven, CT, and London: Yale University Press, 1997.

Sutton, Tina. *The Making of Markova: Diaghilev's Baby Ballerina to Groundbreaking Icon*. New York: Pegasus Books, 2013.

Tallchief, Maria, with Larry Kaplan. *Maria Tallchief: America's Prima Ballerina*. New York: Henry Holt and Company, 1997.

Taper, Bernard. *Balanchine: A Biography*. Second edition. Berkeley, CA: University of California Press, 1996.

Tracy, Robert, and Sharon DeLano. *Balanchine's Ballerinas: Conversations with the Muses*. New York: Linden Press/ Simon & Schuster, 1983.

Vassiliev, Alexandre. Translated by Antonia W. Bouis and Anya Kucharev. *Beauty in Exile: The Artist, Models, and Nobility Who Fled the Russian Revolution and Influenced the World of Fashion*. New York: Harry N. Abrams, 2000.

Volynsky, Akim. *Ballet's Magic Kingdom: Selected Writings on Dance in Russia, 1911–1925*. Translated and edited by Stanley J. Rabinowitz. New Haven, CT, and London: Yale University Press, 2008.

Wilcox, Claire, ed. *The Golden Age of Couture: Paris and London, 1947–1957*. London: V&A Publishing, 2007.

Yohannan, Kohle. *Valentina: American Couture and the Cult of Celebrity*. New York: Rizzoli, 2009.

MAGAZINES

Vogue, 1930–1980

British *Vogue*, 1930–1960

Harper's Bazaar, 1930–1980

Brown and beige net evening gown by Balmain, ca. 1956.

ACKNOWLEDGMENTS

Many assume that writers create publications alone. Though research and writing are indeed solitary endeavors, this book, like the exhibition it accompanies, would not have been possible without the tremendous effort, diligence, expertise, and passion of my colleagues and collaborators. I am deeply grateful to them all.

The project simply could not have happened if it were not for the leadership and support of FIT's President, Joyce F. Brown, and The Museum at FIT's director, Dr. Valerie Steele. Likewise, this book was given life thanks to publisher Mark Magowan of Vendome Press, who understood the potential of *Ballerina*. It is our first collaboration and I am blessed to have had his insight and support from the beginning.

Generous funding for this book was provided by the Fashion Institute of Technology and the Couture Council of The Museum at FIT. Special funding for research and photography in Great Britain was provided by the Janet Arnold Fund of the Society of Antiquaries of London and Theresa McDermott of The Gainsborough Bath Spa.

I am also grateful to my brilliant contributors. For years I have admired the work of Laura Jacobs and Joel Lobenthal. They are among a rare breed of accomplished critics and historians who have contributed to the advancement of both ballet and fashion, and their insights are as moving as the artists and designers they document. I am also thankful for the contributions of fellow museum curators Rosemary Harden of the Bath Fashion Collection in Bath, England, and Jane Pritchard of the Victoria and Albert Museum in London. They have imparted not only their knowledge but also access to collections and material I could have seen nowhere else.

No book is viable without the input and guidance of brilliant editors. I am most fortunate to have had two at my avail throughout the creation of *Ballerina*: Julian Clark of The Museum at FIT and Jacqueline "Jackie" Decter of Vendome Press. Julian has been my long-term partner in prose; everything I produce is made better by him. This is my debut partnership with Jackie, one I have longed for over the years. Working with her has been a dream come true, and far better an experience than I could have hoped for.

As important and insightful as the text of *Ballerina* is, it's the images that give it life. All the gorgeous new photographs are by a trio of talents who brought my vision to life: MFIT's objects are by Eileen Costas; images of the dancers are by Isabel "Issy" Magowan; and Margot Fonteyn's wardrobe was photographed by William "Bill" Palmer, my husband and partner in crime. The mighty task of creating a cohesive book by wedding these new photographs with a plethora of historical images, some of which have seen better days, fell to Susi Oberhelman. Her masterful design breathed life and chicness into the depictions of the glorious ballerinas and fashions illustrated herein.

Obtaining the wide array of historical images was also a herculean task. I am absolutely indebted to MFIT's assistant curator Elizabeth "Liz" Way for all she has done. Liz procured, organized, and captioned all the archival photographs and related images, not only for me but also for all the contributing authors. We simply could not have produced this book without her.

I am also indebted to my colleague fashion journalist and curator Nancy MacDonell for the many hours she spent perusing fashion magazines in search of ballet-inspired fashions and coverage. Thanks to her efforts, *Ballerina* is filled with a wealth of imagery and information.

Many of the objects featured in *Ballerina* were the result of great generosity from an array of expert colleagues. I thank you most profoundly for your support and assistance: Beverley Birks; Hamish Bowles and his curatorial advisor, Molly Sorkin; Oriole Cullen and Edwina Ehrman of the Victoria and Albert Museum; Marc Happel, New York City Ballet's Director of Costumes; Tom Gold of Tom Gold Dance; Tim Long of the Museum of London; and my designer friends and supporters: Behnaz Sarafpour, Victor de Souza, Maggie Norris, and Pierre Cardin.

I wish to thank my wonderful colleagues at The Museum at FIT for their contributions: conservators Ann Coppinger, Alison Castaneda, Marjorie Jonas, and Lauren Posada; registrars Sonia Dingilian and Jill Hemingway; Administrative staff Gladys Rathold, Glendene Small, Lynn Sallaberry, and Gail Bowden; senior curator Fred Dennis and curator of costume and accessories, Colleen Hill; installation guru Tommy Synnamon, who did so much to bring the objects to life; and curator of Special Collections in the FIT Library, April Callahan. I am especially grateful to Nateer Cirino. Though Nateer is officially my assistant, her role is far greater, for she not only handled so many of the financial elements of this book but also provided me with steady support while quietly cheering me on from the sidelines. Thank you, Nateer, my dear friend.

The most important person in my life has been my mother, Myung Kyun Kim Mears, and she was the first person to introduce me to this glorious art form. Born in Korea, she took ballet lessons as a young girl before the outbreak of that nation's civil war and never had a chance to continue her studies after its conclusion. Instead, she gave me the opportunity to learn classical dance. And together we admired an array of ballerinas, from Margot Fonteyn to Cynthia Gregory, to name but two. This book was born from our mutual passion. How can I ever repay you?

Most of all, I must thank the great ballerinas who helped and encouraged me from the start of this project: Sono Osato, Joy Williams Brown, Allegra Kent, Mimi Paul, Veronika Part, Lauren Lovette, and especially my beloved teacher, Patricia "Pat" Heyes Dokoudovsky, and patroness, Carole Divet Harting. These women exemplify the qualities we adore and admire in all ballet artists: beauty, brilliance, charisma, discipline, and grace, as well as generosity and kindness. They are human and superhuman, and they will always be my muses.

PATRICIA MEARS

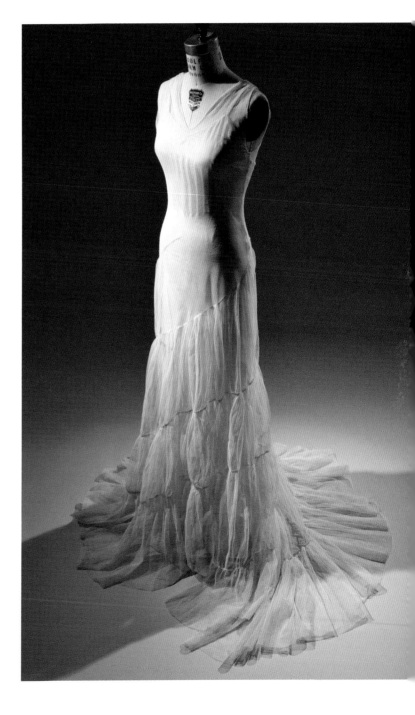

Off-white tulle evening dress by Augustabernard, 1934.

PHOTO CREDITS

© The Irving Penn Foundation | p. 170: Photo by Walter E. Owen. Collection of Joel Lobenthal | p. 173: Photo by George Balanchine. | pp. 174, 187: Photos by John Rawlings | p. 179: Photo by Martha Swope. © Billy Rose Theatre Division, The New York Public Library for the Performing Arts | p. 183: Photo by Hermann Landshoff | p. 185: Photo by Louise Dahl-Wolfe. The Museum at FIT, Gift of Louise Dahl-Wolfe | p. 190: Photo by Fritz Henle | pp. 208, 211: Photos by Bert Stern. Condé Nast via Getty Images | p. 209: Photo by Bert Stern | p. 213: New York World-Telegram and the Sun Newspaper Photograph Collection, Library of Congress, Prints and Photographs Division, LC-USZ62-120876 | p. 214: Photo by Michael Avedon. Courtesy of Mimi Paul | p. 216: Photo by Boris Lipnitzky. Bibliothèque nationale de France | p. 218: Photo by Chris Von Wangenheim. © 2019 The Collection of Chris von Wangenheim, LLC/Licensed by VAGA at Artists Rights Society (ARS), NY | p. 219: Photo by Arthur Elgort. Courtesy of Carole Divet Harting | p. 225: Photo by Andrew Eccles. © Andrew Eccles | Endpapers: Artwork by Irina_QQQ/Shutterstock.com

CHECKLIST OF OBJECTS IN MUSEUM COLLECTIONS

p. 35: The Museum at FIT, P87.20.25 | p. 40: The Museum at FIT, P88.25.3 | p. 43: The Museum at FIT, P86.71.2 | p. 45: The Museum at FIT, 80.1.4. Gift of Florence Anderson and Mary A. Seymour | p. 59: The Museum at FIT, 85.193.5. Gift of Mrs. Varney T. Elliot and Mrs. Rosemary T. Franciscus. | pp. 80–81: The Museum at FIT, 96.117.2. Gift of Irene Averbrook Weissman | p. 85, left: The Museum at FIT, 77.133.2. Gift of Mrs. Hill Montague III; right: The Museum at FIT, 77.89.1. Gift of Mrs. John Hammond | p. 96: The Museum at FIT, 91.241.136. Gift of Robert Wells In Memory of Lisa Kirk | p. 98: The Museum at FIT, 77.89.3. Gift of Mrs. John Hammond | pp. 99 and 150: Fashion Museum Bath, BATMC I.09.338 to B | p. 102: Victoria & Albert Museum, S.301-2001 | p. 105: The Metropolitan Museum of Art, 1974.312.2a, b. Gift of Doris Hakim | p. 108: Chicago History Museum, CC.1974.483. Gift of Mrs. Henry D. Paschen, Jr. | p 109: The Museum at FIT, PL74.1.17. The collection of Mrs. Michael Blankfort | p. 110: Chicago History Museum, 1969.934. Gift of Mrs. Thomas Hart Fisher | p. 111: Fashion Museum Bath, BATMC I.09.823 | p. 115: The Museum at FIT, 76.42.24. Gift of Mrs. John Thomas Trippe | p. 116: The Museum at FIT, 84.125.3. Gift of Mrs. F. Leval | p 117: The Museum at FIT, 84.125.7. Gift of Mrs. F. Leval | pp. 120–21: The Museum at FIT, 91.244.1. Gift of Barbara Louis | p. 122: Victoria & Albert Museum, T.176-1969. Given by Miss Karslake | p. 124: National Gallery of Australia, Canberra, 80.2167.1-2 | p. 129: The Metropolitan Museum of Art, 2016.55a, b | p. 139: Fashion Museum Bath, BATMC I.24.100 & A | pp. 140–41: Fashion Museum Bath, BATMC I.06.127 | p. 143: Fashion Museum Bath, BATMC VI.01.491 & A | p. 144: Fashion Museum Bath, BATMC I.24.43 & A | pp. 146–47: Fashion Museum Bath, BATMC I.09.898 & A | pp. 148–49: Fashion Museum Bath, BATMC I.09.783 | pp. 156–57: Fashion Museum Bath, BATMC I.09.843 & A | pp. 158 and 203: Fashion Museum Bath, BATMC I.09.846 | p. 176: The Museum at FIT,72.61.167. Gift of Mr. and Mrs. Adrian McCardell | p. 182: The Museum at FIT, 72.61.54. Gift of Mr. and Mrs. Adrian McCardell | p. 184: The Museum at FIT, 72.116.1. Gift of Laura Sinderbrand | p. 186: The Museum at FIT, 73.81.1. Gift of Carol Mann | p. 188: The Museum at FIT, 72.61.181. Gift of Mr. and Mrs. Adrian McCardell | p. 189: The Museum at FIT, 72.61.129. Gift of Mr. and Mrs. Adrian McCardell | p. 192: The Museum at FIT, 79.49.73. Gift of Vera Maxwell | p. 193: The Museum at FIT, 79.49.63. Gift of Vera Maxwell | p. 195: The Museum at FIT, 95.180.17. Gift of Igor Kamlukin from the Estate of Valentina Schlee | p. 200: Fashion Museum Bath, BATMC I.09.603 | p. 206: The Museum at FIT, 86.42.5. Gift of Lydia Speir | p. 212: The Museum at FIT, 96.116.3. Gift of Mrs. Michael Batterberry | p. 222: The Museum at FIT, 2007.36.12. Gift of Judith-Ann Corrente | p. 223: The Museum at FIT, 2018.55.5. Gift of Lauren Leichtman | p. 224: The Museum at FIT, 97.61.1. Gift of Geoffrey Beene Inc. | p. 226: The Museum at FIT, 91.36.1. Gift of Carolyne Roehm | p. 228: The Museum at FIT, 2018.59.3. Gift of Carole Divet Harting | p. 229: The Museum at FIT, 2014.63.1. Gift of Anonymous | p. 232: The Museum at FIT, 2005.49.1 | p. 233: The Museum at FIT, 2012.39.1 | p. 234: The Museum at FIT, 2014.35.1. Gift of Christian Louboutin | p. 243, left: The Museum at FIT, 96.112.1. Gift of Lady Arlene Kieta; right: The Museum at FIT, 91.135.6. Gift of Francine Gray | p. 244: The Museum at FIT, 76.106.1. Gift of Mrs. William Randolph Hearst, Jr. | p. 247: The Museum at FIT, 84.125.5. Gift of Mrs. F. Leval | p. 249: The Museum at FIT, 93.71.4. Gift of Mrs. Jessie L. Hills

- *Best efforts were made to verify all photo credits. Any oversight was unintentional and should be brought to the publisher's attention so that it can be corrected in a future printing.*
- *Unless otherwise noted, all photographs are copyright their respective photographers.*

INDEX

TO BALLERINAS

PATRICIA "PAT" HEYES DOKOUDOVSKY

AND

CAROLE DIVET HARTING

Ballerina: Fashion's Modern Muse
First published in 2019 by The Vendome Press
Vendome is a registered trademark of The Vendome Press, LLC

NEW YORK   LONDON
Suite 2043   63 Edith Grove
244 Fifth Avenue   London,
New York, NY 10001   SW10 0LB, UK

www.vendomepress.com

Distributed in North America by Abrams Books
Distributed in the United Kingdom, and the rest of the world, by Thames & Hudson

ISBN 978-0-86565-373-3

Publishers: Beatrice Vincenzini, Mark Magowan, and Francesco Venturi
Editor: Jacqueline Decter
Production Director: Jim Spivey
Prepress Color Manager: Dana Cole
Designer: Susi Oberhelman

Library of Congress Cataloging-in-Publication Data
available upon request

Printed and bound in China by 1010 Printing International Ltd.
First printing

PAGE 1: New York City Ballet (NYCB) ballerina Tanaquil LeClercq in George Balanchine's *La Valse*, 1947. Costume by Barbara Karinska.
PAGE 2: NYCB ballerina Lauren Lovette in a tulle and brocaded evening dress by Behnaz Sarafpour, autumn 2003.
PAGES 3-4: Dovima in Cristóbal Balenciaga's tulle and embroidered satin evening dress. *Harper's Bazaar*, September 1950. Photograph by Richard Avedon.